9/11

50(

CH00329805

1 0 DEC 2(

1 9 MAY 2015

OCT 2013

− 4 FEB 2014

3 0 SEP 2014

− 4 DEC 2014

Thank you for using Derbyshire Libraries.

To renew items, ring Call Derbyshire 08456 058058

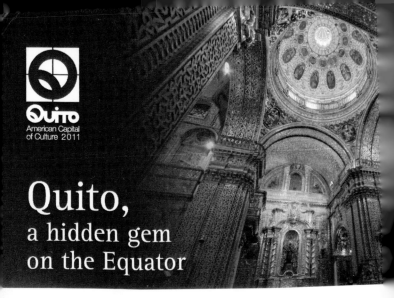

![Quito — American Capital of Culture 2011 logo]

Quito,
a hidden gem
on the Equator

Quito, capital of Ecuador, is located 22 kilometres south of the equator, at 2850 meters (9200 feet) above sea level, on the slopes of Pichincha Volcano.

The entire Metropolitan District of Quito is home to a population of 2.2 million people and enjoys a spring-like temperate climate that ranges from 9 to 20 degrees Celsius.

Quito is an exciting experience along *Latitude 0*, where you can feel the magic of being between two hemispheres at once.

Come to Quito and admire invaluable colonial treasures. The interiors of convents and temples are veritable museums where you can find masterpieces of the Quito School, an artistic movement responsible for the prolific works of colonial Spain.

You will also enjoy delicious local cuisine, shopping for local arts and crafts, as well as adventure tourism on rivers and within mountainous cloud forests, surrounded by butterflies and hummingbirds.

At only an hour's drive from downtown Quito, a 30 meter-tall volcanic rock obelisk topped by a stone globe was erected to mark the equatorial line. Inside, you will find fascinating exhibits that display archaeological artefacts from Ecuador's ageless cultures. **Experience the thrill of the equator's cosmic energy!**

American Capital of Culture 2011

Quito shines its lights on the world as increasing numbers of new visitors come to the city. This year the city was declared American Capital of Culture due to the countless colonial treasures that are found within the city's historic centre: the largest and best preserved in Latin America, with 130 monuments and 5000 landmark buildings, representing 320 hectares of spectacular cultural wealth.

The city is inhabited by a diverse group of people that receive visitors with open arms and a friendly smile. There is always something happening for culture aficionados in Quito - with film festivals, theatre, dance, music performances and art exhibits. **Come and discover Quito's treasures!**

Exciting, traditional and fun

Quito's neighbourhoods are laced with history and tradition, home to magical legends and an inspiring cast of characters, where time seems to have stood still as traditional sports, crafts and practices of old are kept alive and vibrant.

Admire the Historic Centre from the San Juan hillside, indulge in excellent international and local cuisine in La Floresta, walk the train tracks in the valleys of Cumbayá, visit run-down factories that have been converted into stylish museums, ride the mythical train that cuts through the Andes, or enjoy the artistic creativity of Oswaldo Guayasamín.

La Mariscal is where nightlife turns on its party lights. Dancing, music, fun and letting loose come together in Quito's entertainment district, amidst a wide variety of hotels, hostels, restaurants, bars, arts and crafts stores and language schools. A cosmopolitan environment shines through with an exhilarating rainbow of cultural, culinary and artistic options.

Biodiversity and adventure in the outskirts of Quito

Within the city limits or only a few hours from downtown Quito, you can find yourself enjoying jungle excursions or horseback riding at the foot of towering volcanoes. Pump up your adrenaline while mountain biking, trekking, zip-lining, mountain-climbing and white water river-rafting.

Be amazed at the diversity of ecosystems you will find on any route you pick: from the perpetual snow of the highest of Andean peaks to cloud forests, highland lakes, thermal baths and an abundant endemic vegetation and wildlife.

You can travel to Andean marketplaces and remote villages at the foot of the colossal mountains that make up the Avenue of the Volcanoes. **Immerse yourself in nature and adventure!**

More information on the website: **www.quito.com.ec**

Quito®
World Heritage Site

Credits

Footprint credits
Editor: Alan Murphy
Layout and production: Patrick Dawson,
Elysia Alim, Danielle Bricker
Maps: Kevin Feeney

Managing Director: Andy Riddle
Commercial Director: Patrick Dawson
Publisher: Alan Murphy
Publishing Managers: Felicity Laughton,
Nicola Gibbs
Digital Editors: Jo Williams, Tom Mellors
Marketing and PR: Liz Harper
Sales: Diane McEntee
Advertising: Renu Sibal
Finance and Administration: Elizabeth
Taylor

Photography credits
Front cover: Blue-footed booby,
Yai/Shutterstock
Back cover: Quito, XuRa/Shutterstock

Printed in Great Britain by CPI Antony Rowe,
Chippenham, Wiltshire

Publishing information
Footprint *Focus Quito & Galápagos Islands*
1st edition
© Footprint Handbooks Ltd
August 2011

ISBN: 978 1 908206 16 9
CIP DATA: A catalogue record for this book
is available from the British Library

® Footprint Handbooks and the Footprint
mark are a registered trademark of Footprint
Handbooks Ltd

Published by Footprint
6 Riverside Court
Lower Bristol Road
Bath BA2 3DZ, UK
T +44 (0)1225 469141
F +44 (0)1225 469461
footprinttravelguides.com

Distributed in the USA by Globe Pequot Press,
Guilford, Connecticut

FSC
www.fsc.org
FSC®

Every effort has been made
the facts in this guidebook
However, travellers should
advice from consulates, air
travel and visa requiremen
The authors and publisher
responsibility for any loss, injury or
inconvenience however caused.

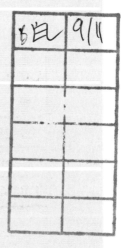

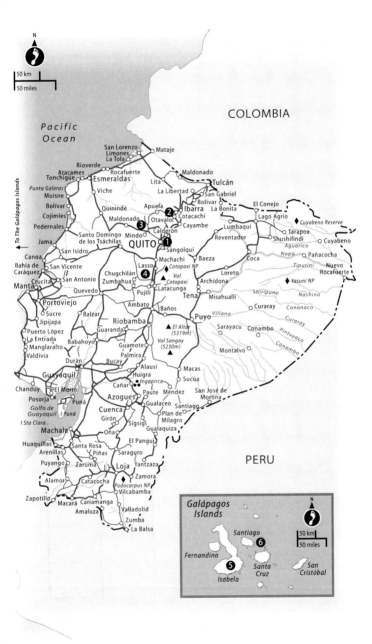

Tucked in between Peru and Colombia, this country is small enough for you to have breakfast with scarlet macaws in the jungle, lunch in the lee of a snow-capped peak and, at tea time, be eyeballed by an iguana whose patch of Pacific beach you have just borrowed.

The capital, Quito, has become one of the gringo centres of South America, bursting at the seams with language schools, travel agencies and restaurants. The smaller towns and villages of Ecuador offer the most authentic experience. Indulge your senses at one of their many markets: dizzying arrays of textiles, ceramics, carvings and other crafts, not to mention the cornucopia of fresh produce.

The exotic wildlife of the Galápagos Islands will also keep you enthralled, whether it's sympathizing with Lonesome George, the last giant tortoise of his race, watching an albatross take off on its flight path, or admiring the sexual paraphernalia of the magnificent frigatebird. If the Galápagos are beyond your budget, then Isla de la Plata is a more accessible alternative for seeing marine life.

Planning your trip

Where to go

The capital, **Quito**, boasts some of the best-preserved colonial architecture in South America in its 'colonial city', while the 'modern Quito' is where you'll find most accommodation, restaurants, tour operators and language schools. From the capital many of the country's attractions are accessible by road in only a few hours. Day trips include nature reserves, hot springs, and, of course, the Equator. There is also good mountaineering and white-water rafting nearby. North of Quito is **Otavalo** with its outstanding handicrafts market, a regular one-day tour, but equally popular as a base for exploring nearby villages, more nature reserves and hiking or cycling routes.

In the Central Sierra, south of Quito is the national park surrounding **Cotopaxi**, one of Ecuador's most frequently climbed volcanoes. Further south is the **Quilotoa circuit**, a 200-km loop through small villages and beautiful landscapes, with lots of possibilities for trekking, cycling and riding. The starting point is Latacunga on the Pan-American Highway.

Ecuador is famous for its **hot springs** and, on either side of the Andes, there is great **birdwatching** in a wide variety of protected areas. Other special interest activities include **diving**, **whitewater rafting** and various **volunteer programmes**. The nature destination par excellence, though, is the **Galápagos Islands**, 970 km west of the mainland. Tours, which are best arranged in Quito, Guayaquil or from home, involve cruising from island to island to see new species with each landfall.

When to go

Ecuador's climate is highly unpredictable. As a general rule, however, in the **Sierra**, there is little variation by day or by season in the temperature: this depends on altitude. The range of shade temperature is from 6°C to 10°C in the morning to 19°C to 23°C in the afternoon, though it can get considerably hotter in the lower basins. Rainfall patterns depend on whether a particular area is closer to the eastern or western slopes of the Andes. To the west, June to September are dry and October to May are wet (but there is sometimes a short dry spell in December or January). To the east, October to February are dry and March to September are wet. There is also variation in annual rainfall from north to south, with the southern highlands being drier. **Quito** is within 25 km of the Equator, but it stands high enough to make its climate much like that of spring in England, the days pleasantly warm and the nights cool. Rainy season is October to May with the heaviest rainfall in April. Rain usually falls in the afternoon. The day length (sunrise to sunset) is almost constant during the year.

Along the **Pacific coast**, rainfall also decreases from north to south, so that it can rain throughout the year in northern Esmeraldas and seldom at all near the Peruvian border. The coast, however, can be enjoyed year-round, although it may be a bit cool from June to November, when mornings are often grey with the *garúa* mists. January to May is the hottest and rainiest time of the year. Like the coast the **Galápagos** suffer from the *garúa* from May to December; from January to April the islands are hottest and brief but heavy showers can fall. In the **Oriente**, heavy rain can fall at any time, but it is usually wettest from March to September.

Ecuador's **high season** is from June to early September, which is also the best time for climbing and trekking. There is also a short tourist season in December and January. In resort areas at major fiestas, such as Carnival, Semana Santa and over New Year, accommodation can be hard to find. Hotels will be full in individual towns during their particular festivals, but Ecuador as a whole is not overcrowded at any time of the year.

Getting there

The vast majority of international flights to Ecuador arrive at **Quito** (UIO, page 18). The busy seasons are 7 December-15 January and 10 July-10 September. If you intend travelling during those times, book as far ahead as possible. From February to May and September to November special offers may be available.

Flights from Europe
From the UK flights to Quito start at £605 (return, low season 2010 prices). Direct flights are available from Madrid or Barcelona with **Iberia** and **LAN** and from Amsterdam with **KLM**. Most connecting flights in Europe are through these cities although it is possible to fly to the USA and get a connecting flight with one of the carriers shown below. It is also possible to fly direct to other South American cities and then get a connecting flight onward to Quito.

From the USA and Canada
From the USA (Miami), return flights to Quito start at around US$460. Quito can be reached directly from Miami, Houston, Atlanta and New York with **American**, **LAN**, **Delta**, **AeroGal** and **Continental Airlines**. Flights from all other US and Canadian cities must go via these destinations.

Departure tax
When you buy your ticket, always check whether departure tax is included. International departure tax is US$40.80 from Quito, payable in cash only, US dollars or local currency. You will not be allowed to board the plane without proof of payment.

Getting around

Air TAME ① *reservations: T1-800-500800 or 02-397 7100, www.tame.com.ec*, is the main internal airline, flying to all major airports and the Galápagos. Enquire locally for up-to-date routes and timetables as they change constantly. TAME offices are listed under each relevant town or city. Smaller airlines include **Aerogal** ① *T1-800-237642 or 02-294 2800, www.aerogal.com.ec*, flies from Quito to Guayaquil, Cuenca, Manta and the Galápagos; **Icaro** ① *T1-800-883567, www.icaro.aero*, flies from Quito to Guayaquil, Manta and Coca. **LAN** ① *T1-800-101075, www.lan.com*, serves Quito, Guayaquil and Cuenca; **Saereo** ① *T1-800-723736 or 02-330 2280, www.saereo.com*, flies from Quito to Macas and Machala, and from Guayaquil to Loja; **VIP** ① *contact through Aerogal*, flies from Quito to Lago Agrio and Coca.

Bus Bus travel is generally more convenient and regular than in other Andean countries. Several companies use comfortable air-conditioned buses on their longer routes; some companies have their own stations, away from the main bus terminals, exclusively for these better buses. **Note** Throughout Ecuador, travel by bus is safest during the daytime.

Hitchhiking Public transport in Ecuador is so abundant that there is seldom any need to hitchhike along the major highways. On small out-of-the-way country roads however, the situation can be quite the opposite, and giving passers-by a ride is common practice and safe, especially in the back of a pick-up or truck. A small fee is usually charged, check in advance.

Train Empresa de Ferrocarriles Ecuatorianos ① *www.efe.gov.ec*. A few segments of the spectacular Ecuadorean railway system have been restored. In 2010, tourist rides were being offered: from **Riobamba to Sibambe**, from **Quito to Latacunga** via Parque Nacional Cotopaxi, from **Ibarra to Primer Paso** and from **El Tambo to Baños del Inca**.

Maps and guide books Instituto Geográfico Militar (IGM) ① *Senierges y Telmo Paz y Miño, on top of the hill to the east of Parque El Ejido. From Av 12 de Octubre, opposite the Casa de la Cultura, take Jiménez (a small street) up the hill. Cross Av Colombia and continue uphill on Paz y Miño behind the Military Hospital, then turn right to the guarded main entrance. You have to deposit your passport or identification card. T02-397 5100, ext 2502, www.igm.gov.ec. Map sales room open Mon-Fri 0800-1600.* They sell country maps and topographic maps, covering most areas of Ecuador, in various scales, original, US$2, colour copy (pick-up next day), US$3.36, colour plotted copy US$3.08 (1-hour wait). Maps of border areas and the seacoast are 'reservado' (classified) and not available for sale without a military permit (requires extra time). Buy your maps here, they are rarely available outside Quito. Map and geographic reference libraries are located next to the sales room. There is a beautiful view from the grounds. Two recommended road atlases, *Guía Vial* and *Guía de Quito*, published by **Ediguías** in Quito, are available in book shops. Online maps of major Ecuadorean cities are found on www.guiame.com.ec.

Sleeping

Hotels Outside the provincial capitals and a few resorts, there are few higher-class hotels, although a number of *haciendas* have opened their doors to paying guests. A few are in the Exclusive Hotels & Haciendas of Ecuador group ① *Av 12 de Octubre E11-14 y Orellana, Edif Lincoln, p 2, T02-254 4719, www.ehhec.com*, but there are many other independent haciendas of good quality. Some are mentioned in the text. Larger towns and tourist centres often have more hotels than we can list. This is especially true of Quito. The hotels that are included are among the best in each category, selected to provide a variety of locations and styles. Service of 10% and tax of 12% are added to better hotel and restaurant bills. Some cheaper hotels apply the 12% tax, but check if it is included. Many hotel rooms have very low wattage bulbs, keen readers are advised to take a head torch.

Camping Camping in protected natural areas can be one of the most satisfying experiences during a visit to Ecuador. Organized campsites, car or trailer camping on the other hand are virtually unheard-of. Because of the abundance of cheap hotels you should never *have to* camp in Ecuador, except for cyclists who may be stuck between towns. In this case the best strategy is to ask permission to camp on someone's private land, preferably within sight of their home for safety. It is not safe to pitch your tent at random near villages

Sleeping and eating price codes

Sleeping

$$$$ over US$150   **$$$** US$66-150   **$$** US$30-65
$ Under US$30
Price codes refer to the cost of two people sharing a double room in the high season.

Eating

$$$ over US$12   **$$** US$6-12   **$** under US$6
Prices refer to the average cost of a two-course meal for one person, not including drinks or service charge.

and even less so on beaches. *Bluet Camping Gas* is easily obtainable, but white gas, like US Coleman fuel, is hard to find. Unleaded petrol (gasoline) is available everywhere and may be an alternative for some stoves.

Eating and drinking

Eating out Upmarket restaurants add 22% to the bill, 12% tax plus 10% service. All other places add the 12% tax, which is also charged on non-essential items in food shops. The cuisine varies with region. The following are some typical dishes.

Throughout the country If economizing ask for the set meal in restaurants, *almuerzo* at lunch time, *merienda* in the evening – very cheap and wholesome; it costs US$2-3. *Fanesca*, a fish soup with beans, many grains, ground peanuts and more, sold in Easter Week, is very filling (it is so popular that in Quito and main tourist spots it is sold throughout Lent). *Ceviche*, marinated fish or seafood which is usually served with popcorn and roasted maize (*tostado*), is very popular throughout Ecuador. Only *ceviche de pescado* (fish) and *ceviche de concha* (clams) which are marinated raw, potentially pose a health hazard. The other varieties of *ceviche* such as *camarón* (shrimp/prawn) and *langostino* (jumbo shrimp/king prawn) all of which are cooked before being marinated, are generally safe (check the cleanliness of the establishment). *Langosta* (lobster) is an increasingly endangered species but continues to be illegally fished; please be conscientious. Ecuadorean food is not particularly spicy. However, in most homes and restaurants, the meal is accompanied by a small bowl of *ají* (hot pepper sauce) which may vary in potency. *Colada* is a generic name which can refer to cream soups or sweet beverages. In addition to the prepared foods mentioned above, Ecuador offers a large variety of delicious fruits, some of which are unique to South America.

Drink The best fruit drinks are *naranjilla*, *maracuyá* (passion fruit), *tomate de árbol*, *piña* (pineapple), *taxo* (another variety of passion fruit) and *mora* (blackberry), but note that fruit juices are sometimes made with unboiled water. Main beers available are *Pilsener*, *Club*, and *Brahma*. Argentine and Chilean wines are available in the larger cities. Good *aguardiente* (unmatured rum, *Cristal* is recommended), also known as *puntas, trago de caña*, or just *trago*. The usual soft drinks, known as *colas*, are available. Instant coffee or liquid concentrate is common, so ask for *café pasado* if you want real coffee. In tourist centres and many upscale hotels and restaurants, good cappuccino and espresso can be found.

Essentials A-Z

Accident and emergency

Emergency telephone numbers:
T911 in Quito and Cuenca, T112 in Guayaquil,
T101 for police everywhere.

Electricity

AC throughout, 110 volts, 60 cycles.
Sockets are for twin flat blades, sometimes
with a round earth pin.

Embassies and consulates

For a complete list of Ecuadorean embassies
and consulates, visit www.mmrree.gov.ec.

Festivals and events

1 Jan: New Year's Day; **6 Jan**: Reyes Magos
y Día de los Inocentes, a time for pranks,
which closes the Christmas-New Year
holiday season. **27 Fe**b: Día del Civismo,
celebrating the victory over Peru at Tarqui
in 1829. **Carnival**: Mon and Tue before Lent,
celebrated everywhere in the Andes, except
Ambato, by throwing water at passers-by:
be prepared to participate. **Easter**: Holy Thu,
Good Fri, Holy Sat. **1 May**: Labour Day; **24
May**: Battle of Pichincha, Independence.
Early Jun: Corpus Christi. **10 Aug**: first
attempt to gain the Independence of Quito. **9
Oct**: Independence
of Guayaquil. **2 Nov**: All Souls' Day. **3 Nov**:
Independence of Cuenca. **1-6 Dec**:
Foundation of Quito. **25 Dec**: Christmas
Day.

Money → *US$1=€0.69 (Jun 2011).*

The **US dollar** (US$) is the official currency of
Ecuador. Only US$ bills circulate. US coins are
used alongside the equivalent size and value
Ecuadorean coins. Ecuadorean coins have no
value outside the country. Many
establishments are reluctant to accept bills
larger than US$20 because of counterfeit
notes or lack of change. There is no substitute
for cash-in-hand when travelling in Ecuador.
Euros are slowly gaining acceptance, but US$
cash in small denominations is by far the
simplest and the only universally accepted
option. Other currencies are difficult to
exchange outside large cities and fetch a
very poor rate.

Plastic/traveller's cheques/banks/ATMs The
most commonly accepted **credit cards** are
Visa, MasterCard, Diners and, to a lesser extent,
American Express. Cash advances on credit
cards can be obtained through many ATMs
(only Banco de Guayaquil for Amex), but daily
limits apply. Larger advances on Visa and
MasterCard are available from the main
branches of the following banks: **Banco
Bolivariano, Banco de Guayaquil** (Visa only),
Banco del Austro and **Banco del Pacífico**.
Paying by credit card may incur a surcharge (at
least 10%). TCs are not accepted by most
merchants, hotels or tour agencies in Ecuador.
They can be exchanged for cash at **Banco del
Pacífico** (main branches) and some **casas de
cambio** including Vaz Corp (in Quito, Otavalo,
Guayaquil, Cuenca, Loja and Machala). A
passport is always required to exchange TCs.
American Express is the most widely accepted
brand, but they are no longer replaced in
Ecuador; if they are lost or stolen, you must file
a claim from home. A police report is required
if TCs are stolen. Internationally linked **ATMs**
are common, although they cannot always be
relied on. Debit cards are less easy to use. ATMs
are a focus for scams and robberies, use them
judiciously. Funds may be rapidly wired to
Ecuador by **Western Union**, high fees and
taxes apply.

Cost of living/travelling Despite
dollarization, prices remain modest by
international standards and Ecuador is still
affordable for even the budget traveller.
A very basic daily travel budget in 2010 was
US$15-20 per person based on two travelling

together, but allow for higher costs in Quito and Guayaquil. For US$50 a day you can enjoy a good deal of comfort. Internet use is about US$0.60-1 per hour. An **International Student Identity Card** (**ISIC**) may help you obtain discounts when travelling. ISIC cards are sold in Quito by **Idiomas Travel** ① *Roca 130 y 12 de Octubre, p 2, T250 0264, www.idiomas.com.ec*. They need proof of full-time enrolment in Ecuador or abroad (minimum 20 hrs/week), 2 photos and US$15.

Opening hours

Banks open Mon-Fri 0900-1600. **Government offices** variable hours Mon-Fri, but most close for lunch. **Other offices** 0900-1230, 1430-1800. **Shops** 0900-1900; close at midday in smaller towns, open till 2100 on the coast.

Safety

Urban street crime, bag snatching and slashing, and robbery along the country's highways are the most significant hazards. In an effort to fight crime, army and police patrols operate in some cities and along some highways. Don't be taken aback to see these troops on duty. Secure your belongings, be wary of con tricks, avoid crowds and travel only during the daytime. The countryside and small towns are generally safest, but theft and robbery have been reported from several places where tourists gather. It is the big cities, Guayaquil, Quito, Santo Domingo, and to a lesser extent Cuenca, which call for the greatest care. The northern border with Colombia, including the provinces of Esmeraldas, Carchi, and especially Sucumbíos, call for additional precautions. Armed conflict in Colombia has caused an influx of refugees, and parts of these provinces have come under the influence of insurgents. Enquire locally before travelling to and in any northern border areas.

Occasional social unrest is part of life in Ecuador and you should not overreact.

Strikes and protests are usually announced days or weeks in advance, and their most significant impact on tourists is the restriction of overland travel.

Tourist information

Ministerio de Turismo ① *Eloy Alfaro N32-300 y Carlos Tobar, Quito, T02-250 7559, www.ecuador.travel*. Local offices are given in the text. The ministry has a Public Prosecutors Office (Fiscalía, T ext 1018) where serious complaints should be reported. Outside Ecuador, tourist information can be obtained from Ecuadorean Embassies. National parks, of which Ecuador has an outstanding array, are controlled by the **Ministerio del Ambiente** ① *Edificio MAG, p 8, Amazonas y Eloy Alfaro, Quito, T02-250 6337*. The ministry has less information than the park offices in the cities nearest the parks themselves.

Tax

Airport tax International flights at Quito airport US$40.80; at Guayaquil it is US$28.27. 12% tax on air tickets for flights originating in Ecuador. Domestic airport tax of US$7.60 (for Quito) is included in the ticket price. **VAT/IVA** 12%. Taxes on imported luxury items are high.

Telephone

International phone code: +593. **Note** Many non-Ecuadorean mobile phone networks cannot connect in Quito. Outside the capital, connectivity is a little better, but for local use, buy an Ecuadorean chip (US$3-5).

Time

Official time is GMT -5 (Galápagos, -6).

Tipping

In restaurants 10% may be included in the bill. In cheaper restaurants, tipping is uncommon but welcome. It is not expected in taxis. Airport porters, US$0.50-1, according to number of cases.

Visas and immigration

All visitors to Ecuador must have a passport valid for at least 6 months and an onward or return ticket. The latter is seldom asked for. Visas are not required for tourists, regardless of nationality, unless they wish to stay more than 90 days. Upon entry all visitors must complete an international embarkation/disembarkation card. Keep your copy, you will be asked for it when you leave.

Note You are required by Ecuadorean law to carry your passport at all times. Whether or not a photocopy is an acceptable substitute is at the discretion of the individual police officer. In addition, travellers must carry an **international vaccination certificate**, although the latter is almost never asked for. Tourists are not permitted to work under any circumstances.

Length of stay Tourists are granted 90 days upon arrival and there are no extensions except for citizens of the Andean Community of Nations. Visitors staying over 90 days will be fined US$200. The fine must be payed 48 hrs prior to departure at a *jefatura provincial* (provincial head-quarters)

of the **Policía Nacional de Migración** (www.migracion.gov.ec), most are located in provincial capitals; in Quito, **Jefatura Provincial de Migración de Pichincha** ⓘ *Amazonas 171 y República, T227 6394, open Mon-Fri 0800-1200 and 1500-1800*. The maximum stay is 90 days per 12 month period. Visitors will not be allowed back in the country if they have already stayed for 90 days. If you want to spend more time studying, volunteering etc, you can get a purpose specific visa ('12/9' category) at the end of your 90 days as a tourist.

Visas for longer stays are issued by the **Ministerio de Relaciones Exteriores** (Foreign Office, www.mmrree.gov.ec), through their diplomatic representatives abroad and administered in Quito by the **Dirección General de Asuntos Migratorios** (non-immigrant visas) and the **Dirección Nacional de Extranjería** (immigrant visas).

Weights and measures

Metric, US gallons for petrol, some English measures for hardware and weights and some Spanish measures for weights.

Contents

Footprint features

Quito & around

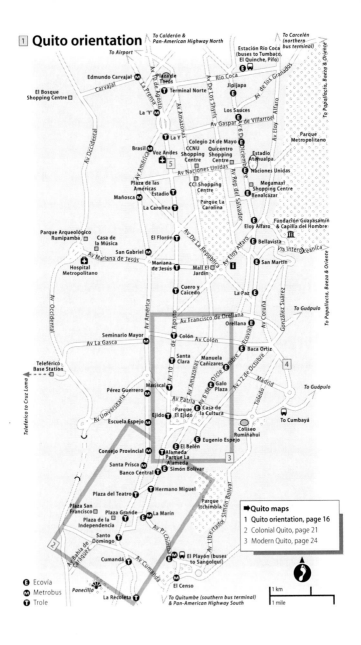

1 Quito orientation

To Calderón & Pan-American Highway North

To Airport

To Carcelén (northern bus terminal)

Estación Río Coca (buses to Tumbaco, El Quinche, Pifo)

El Bosque Shopping Centre

Edmundo Carvajal Ⓜ

Plaza de Toros

Terminal Norte

Río Coca

Jipijapa

Los Sauces

La 'Y'

Av Gaspar de Villarroel

La 'Y' Ⓣ

Colegio 24 de Mayo

Brasil Ⓜ

Voz Andes

CCNU Shopping Centre

Quicentro Shopping Centre

Estadio Atahualpa

Naciones Unidas

Av Naciones Unidas

Megamaxi Shopping Centre

Plaza de las Américas

CCI Shopping Centre

Benalcázar

Estadio Ⓣ

Mañosca Ⓜ

Parque La Carolina

La Carolina Ⓣ

Parque Arqueológico Rumipamba

Casa de la Música

Eloy Alfaro

Fundación Guayasamín & Capilla del Hombre

El Florón Ⓣ

San Gabriel Ⓜ

San Gabriel

Av Mariana de Jesús

Mariana de Jesús Ⓣ

Bellavista

Hospital Metropolitano

Mall El Jardín

San Martín

Cuero y Caicedo

La Paz

Teleférico Base Station

Seminario Mayor

Av Francisco de Orellana

Orellana

Av La Gasca

Colón Ⓣ Av Colón

Baca Ortiz

Santa Clara Ⓣ

Manuela Cañizares

Pérez Guerrero

Mariscal Ⓣ Ⓜ

Galo Plaza

Madrid

To Guápulo

Av Patria

Casa de la Cultura

Toledo

Parque El Ejido

Ejido Ⓣ

To Cumbayá

Escuela Espejo Ⓜ

Eugenio Espejo

Coliseo Rumiñahui

Consejo Provincial Ⓜ

El Belén Ⓣ

Alameda Parque La Alameda

Santa Prisca Ⓜ

Banco Central Ⓔ Simón Bolívar

Plaza del Teatro Ⓣ

Hermano Miguel Ⓣ

Parque Itchimbía

Plaza San Francisco

Plaza Grande

La Marín

Plaza de la Independencia

Av Pichincha

Santo Domingo

El Playón (buses to Sangolquí)

Cumandá Ⓣ

Av Cumandá

El Censo

Panecillo

La Recoleta Ⓣ

To Quitumbe (southern bus terminal) & Pan-American Highway South

Ⓔ Ecovía

Ⓜ Metrobus

Ⓣ Trole

➡ Quito maps
1 Quito orientation, page 16
2 Colonial Quito, page 21
3 Modern Quito, page 24

1 km
1 mile

Quito

Few cities have a setting to match that of Quito, the second highest capital in Latin America after La Paz. The city is set in a hollow at the foot of the volcano Pichincha (4794 m). The city's charm lies in its colonial centre – the Centro Histórico as it's known – a UNESCO World Heritage Site, where cobbled streets are steep and narrow, dipping to deep ravines. From the top of Cerro Panecillo, 183 m above the city level, there is a fine view of the city below and the encircling cones of volcanoes and other mountains.

North of the colonial centre is modern Quito with broad avenues lined with contemporary office buildings, fine private residences, parks, embassies and villas. Here you'll find Quito's main tourist area in the district known as La Mariscal, bordered by Avenidas Amazonas, Patria, 12 de Octubre and Orellana.

Ins and outs → *Phone code: 02. Population: 1,700,000. Altitude: 2850 m.*

Getting there Mariscal Sucre airport is about 5 km north of the main hotel district. It is served by taxis (US$6 to La Mariscal, US$8 to colonial Quito, recommended as the safest option), the *Trole* and *Metrobus* transit systems and city buses. Long-distance bus services leave from terminals at the extreme edges of the city, Quitumbe in the south and Carcelén in the north. It is safest to arrive and leave terminals by taxi, although both terminals are served by public transit systems. Some bus services run to their own offices in modern Quito. ▸▸ *See also Transport, page 43.*

Getting around Both colonial Quito and La Mariscal in modern Quito can be explored on foot, but getting between the two requires some form of public transport, which is plentiful and usually slow. Using taxis is the best option, as it's convenient and cheap (starting at US$1); authorized taxis display a unit number, driver's photograph and have a meter. There are city buses and three parallel transit lines running north to south on exclusive lanes: the *Trole*, *Ecovía* and *Metrobus*. Public transit is not designed for carrying heavy luggage and is often crowded. Quito's main arteries run north-south and traffic congestion along them is a serious problem. Avenida Occidental is a somewhat more expedite road to the west of the city. The Corredor Periférico Oriental is a bypass to the east of the city running 44 km between Santa Rosa in the south and Calderón in the north. Roads through the eastern suburbs in the Valle de los Chillos and Tumbaco can be taken to avoid the city proper. **Note** There are vehicular restrictions on weekdays 0700-0930 and 1600-1930, based on the last digit of the licence plate. Colonial Quito is closed to vehicles Sunday 0900-1600.

Orientation Most places of historical interest are in colonial Quito, while the majority of the hotels, restaurants, travel agencies and facilities for visitors are in the modern city to the north. The street numbering system is based on N (Norte), E (Este), S (Sur), Oe (Oeste), plus a number for each street and a number for each building, however, an older system of street numbers is also still in use. Note that, because of Quito's altitude and notorious air pollution, some visitors may feel some discomfort: slow your pace for the first 48 hours.

Tourist information Empresa Metropolitana Quito Turismo/Quito Visitor's Bureau ① *T299 3300, www.quito.com.ec*, has information offices with English-speaking personnel, brochures and maps, and an excellent website. They also run walking tours of the colonial city, see Paseos Culturales, page 38. **Airport:** International Arrivals ① *T330 0163, daily 0900-2400;* **National Arrivals** ① *T330 0164, daily 0800-1600.* **Bus station:** Terminal Quitumbe ① *daily 0800-1800.* **Colonial Quito:** Plaza de la Independencia ① *El Quinde craft shop at Palacio Municipal, Venezuela y Espejo, T257 2445, Mon-Fri 0900-1930, Sat 0900-1900, Sun 1000-1700;* La Ronda ① *Casa de las Artes, Morales 999 y Venezuela, Tue-Sat 0900-1700;* Plaza de San Francisco ① *kiosk at Benalcázar y Sucre, Tue-Fri 0900-1700, Sat-Sun 1000-1600.* **Modern Quito:** Museo del Banco Central ① *Av Patria y 6 de Diciembre, T222 1116, Tue-Fri 0900-1700, Sat and Sun 1000-1600;* Galería Ecuador ① *Reina Victoria N24-263 y García, T223 9469, Tue-Sun 1000-2200,* in gourmet food shop and café.

The **Ministerio de Turismo** ① *Eloy Alfaro N32-300 (between República and Shyris), T256 5947, www.ecuador.travel, Mon-Fri 0830-1700,* has an information counter with brochures, some staff speak English. **South American Explorers** ① *Jorge Washington 311 y Leonidas Plaza, T222 5228, quitoclub@saexplorers.org, Mon-Fri 0930-1700, Sat 0900-1200.* Members may receive post and faxes, use internet and store gear. Local discounts with SAE card. They also organize weekend excursions for members.

Safety Like any big city, Quito requires precautions. The authorities are working on improving public safety and some areas, like the colonial centre, are now safer, but theft and armed robbery remain hazards. In colonial Quito, Plaza de la Independencia and La Ronda are patrolled by officers from the **Policía Metropolitana** who speak some English and are very helpful. El Panecillo is patrolled by neighbourhood brigades (see page 22). In modern Quito, efforts are being made to make La Mariscal district safer, but vigilance is necessary here at all hours. Plaza El Quinde (Calle Foch y Reina Victoria) in La Mariscal is also patrolled. Watch your belongings at all times, do not carry unnecessary valuables, avoid crowds and especially crowded public transit. Use taxis at night and whenever you carry valuables. Be extra careful after 2200, especially in La Mariscal. Bag slashing can be a problem at bus stops, especially La Marín. Do not walk through any city parks in the evening or even in daylight at quiet times. There have also been reports of scams on long distance buses leaving Quito, especially to Baños; do not give your hand luggage to anyone and always keep your things on your lap, not in the overhead storage rack nor on the floor. The **Policía de Turismo** ① *HQ at Reina Victoria N21-208 y Roca, T254 3983, open 0800-1800 for information, 24 hrs for emergencies, offices at Plaza de la Independencia, Pasaje Arzobispal, Chile y García Moreno, T251 0896, 1000-1800, and at the airport, near international arrivals, T294 4900 ext 2360, 0800-1800,* offers information and is one place to obtain a police report in case of theft.

Sights

Colonial Quito → *For listings see pages 27-49.*

Quito's revitalized colonial district is a pleasant place to stroll and admire the architecture, monuments and art. At night, the illuminated plazas and churches are very beautiful. The heart of the old city is **Plaza de la Independencia** or **Plaza Grande**, whose pink-flowered arupo trees bloom in September. It is dominated by a somewhat grim **cathedral** ① *entry through museum, Venezuela N3-117, T257 0371, Mon-Sat 0930-1600, no entry during Mass, US$1.50 for the museum, night visits to church and cupolas on request,* built 1550-1562, with grey stone porticos and green tile cupolas. On its outer walls are plaques listing the names of the founding fathers of Quito, and inside are the tomb of Sucre and a famous Descent from the Cross by the indigenous painter Caspicara. There are many other 17th- and 18th-century paintings; the interior decoration shows Moorish influence. Facing the Cathedral is the **Palacio Arzobispal**, part of which now houses shops. Next to it, in the northwest corner, is the **Hotel Plaza Grande** (1930), with a baroque façade, the first building in the old city with more than two storeys. On the northeast side is the concrete **Municipio**, which fits in quite well. The low colonial **Palacio de Gobierno** or **Palacio de Carondelet**, silhouetted against the flank of Pichincha, is on the northwest side of the Plaza. On the first floor is a gigantic mosaic mural of Orellana navigating the Amazon. The ironwork on the balconies looking over the main plaza is from the Tuilleries in Paris. With the government motto "Ahora Carondelet es de todos", visitors can take **tours** ① *T258 4000, ex 218, Tue-Sun 0900-1130, 1300-1615, take passport or copy.*

From Plaza de la Independencia two main streets, Venezuela and García Moreno, lead straight towards the Panecillo. Parallel with Venezuela is Calle Guayaquil, the main shopping street. These streets all run south from the main plaza to meet Calle Morales, better known as **La Ronda**, one of the oldest streets in the city. This narrow cobbled pedestrian way and its colonial homes with wrought-iron balconies have been refurbished and house restaurants, bars, cultural centres and shops. It is a quaint corner of the city growing in popularity for a night out or an afternoon stroll. On García Moreno N3-94 is the beautiful **El Sagrario** ① *daily, 0700-1800, no entry during Mass, free,* church with a gilded door. The **Centro Cultural Metropolitano** is at the corner of Espejo, housing the municipal library, a museum for the visually impaired, temporary exhibits and the **Museo Alberto Mena Caamaño** ① *entry on C Espejo, T258 4362 ext 135, www.centro cultural-quito.com, Tue-Sun 0900-1630, US$1.50.* This wax museum depicts scenes of Ecuadorean colonial history. The scene of the execution of the revolutionaries of 1809 in the original cell is particularly vivid. The fine Jesuit church of **La Compañía** ① *García Moreno N3-117 y Sucre, T258 4175, www.ficj.org.ec, Mon-Fri 0930-1730, Sat and holidays 09300-1630, Sun 1330-1630, US$2,* has the most ornate and richly sculptured façade and interior. Many of its most valuable treasures are in vaults at the Banco Central. Diagonally opposite is the **Casa Museo María Augusta Urrutia** ① *García Moreno N2-60 y Sucre, T258 0103, Tue-Fri 1000-1800, Sat-Sun 0930-1730, US$2.00,* the home of a Quiteña who devoted her life to charity, showing the lifestyle of 20th-century aristocracy.

Housed in the fine restored, 16th century Hospital San Juan de Dios, is the **Museo de la Ciudad** ① *García Moreno 572 y Rocafuerte, T228 3882, www.museociudadquito.gov.ec,*

② Colonial Quito

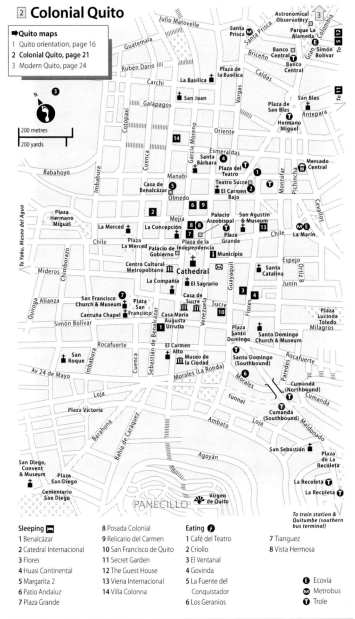

➡Quito maps
1 Quito orientation, page 16
2 **Colonial Quito, page 21**
3 Modern Quito, page 24

200 metres
200 yards

Sleeping 🛏
1 Benalcázar
2 Catedral Internacional
3 Flores
4 Huasi Continental
5 Margarita 2
6 Patio Andaluz
7 Plaza Grande
8 Posada Colonial
9 Relicario del Carmen
10 San Francisco de Quito
11 Secret Garden
12 The Guest House
13 Viena Internacional
14 Villa Colonna

Eating 🍴
1 Café del Teatro
2 Criollo
3 El Ventanal
4 Govinda
5 La Fuente del Conquistador
6 Los Geranios
7 Tianguez
8 Vista Hermosa

🅔 Ecovía
Ⓜ Metrobus
🅣 Trole

Tue-Sun 0930-1730, US$3, foreign language guide service US$6 per group (request ahead). It takes you through Quito's history from prehispanic times to the 19th century, with imaginative displays.

On **Cerro Panecillo** ① *Mon-Thu 0900-1700, Fri-Sun 0900-2100, US$1 per vehicle or US$0.25 per person if walking, for the neighbourhood safety brigade; entry to the interior of the monument US$2,* there is a statue of the Virgen de Quito and a good view from the observation platform. Although the neighbourhood patrols the area, it is safer to take a taxi (US$6 return from the colonial city, US$10 from La Mariscal, with a short wait). In the museum of the monastery of **San Diego** ① *Calicuchima 117 y Farfán, entrance to the right of the church, T295 2516, 0930-1300, 1430-1730 daily, US$2* (by the cemetery of the same name, just west of Panecillo), guided tours (Spanish only) take you around four colonial patios where sculpture and painting are shown. Of special interest are the gilded pulpit by Juan Bautista Menacho and the Last Supper painting in the refectory, in which a *cuy* and *humitas* have taken the place of the paschal lamb.

Plaza de San Francisco (or Bolívar) is west of Plaza de la Independencia; here are the great church and monastery of the patron saint of Quito, **San Francisco** ① *Mon-Sat 0900-1200, 1500-1700, Sun 0900-1200.* The church was constructed by the Spanish in 1553 and is rich in art treasures. A modest statue of the founder, Fray Jodoco Ricke, the Flemish Franciscan who sowed the first wheat in Ecuador, stands at the foot of the stairs to the church portal. See the fine wood-carvings in the choir, a high altar of gold and an exquisite carved ceiling. There are some paintings in the aisles by Miguel de Santiago, the colonial *mestizo* painter. The **Museo Franciscano Fray Pedro Gocial** ① *Cuenca 477 y Sucre, T228 1124, Mon-Fri 0900-1300, 1400-1800, Sat 0900-1800, Sun 0900-1300, US$2,* has a collection of religious art. Adjoining San Francisco is the **Cantuña Chapel** ① *0800-1700,* with sculptures. Not far away to the north along Calle Cuenca is the church of **La Merced** ① *entrance on C Chile, 0630-1200, 1400-1800, free,* with many splendidly elaborate styles.

At **Plaza de Santo Domingo** (or Sucre), southeast of Plaza de la Independencia, is the church and monastery of **Santo Domingo**, with its rich wood-carvings and a remarkable Chapel of the Rosary to the right of the main altar. In the monastery is the **Museo Dominicano Fray Pedro Bedón** ① *T228 0518, Tue-Sun 1000-1700, US$2,* another fine collection of religious art. In the centre of the plaza is a statue of Sucre, pointing to the slopes of Pichincha where he won his battle against the Royalists. Nearby is the **Museo Casa de Sucre** ① *Venezuela N3-117 y Sucre, T295 2860, Mon-Fri 0930-1630, Sat-Sun 1000-1600, US$1,* a military museum in the beautiful house of Sucre.

Museo de Santa Catalina ① *Espejo 779 y Flores, T228 4000, Mon-Fri 0830-1700, Sat 0830-1200, US$1.50,* said to have been built on the ruins of the Inca House of the Virgins, depicts the history of cloistered life. Many of the heroes of Ecuador's struggle for independence are buried in the monastery of **San Agustín** (Flores y Chile), which has beautiful cloisters on three sides where the first act of independence from Spain was signed on 10 August 1809. Here is the **Museo Miguel de Santiago** ① *Chile 924 y Guayaquil, T295 5225, www.migueldesantiago.com, Mon-Fri 0900-1230, 1430-1700, Sat 0900-1300, US$1,* with religious art.

The **Basílica** ① *on Plaza de la Basílica, Carchi 122 y Venezuela, northeast of Plaza de la Independencia, T228 9428, Mon-Sat 0930-1730, Sun 0900-1300, US$2,* is very large, has many gargoyles (some in the shape of Ecuadorean fauna), stained glass windows and fine, bas relief bronze doors (begun in 1926; some final details remain unfinished due to lack of funding). A coffee shop in the clock tower gives good views over the city. The **Centro de Arte Contemporáneo** ① *Luis Dávila y Venezuela, San Juan, T398 8800, Tue-Sun 0900-1600, US$2*, in the beautifully restored Antiguo Hospital Militar, built in the early 1900s, has an exhibition on the Quito Revolution (www.revolucionquito.com) in place till end-2010. To the west of the city, the **Yaku Museo del Agua** ① *El Placer Oe11-271, T257 0359, www.yakumuseoagua.gov.ec, Tue-Sat 0900-1700, Sun 0900-1700, US$3*, has great views of the city. Its main themes are water and nature, society and heritage; great for children. The best way there is take a taxi or walk up Calle Chile, go under the tunnels road then left to El Placer. East of the colonial city is **Parque Itchimbía** ① *T228 2017, www.parque itchimbia.org.ec*; a natural look-out over the city with walking and cycle trails and a cultural centre housed in a 19th-century 'crystal palace' which came from Europe, once housed the Santa Clara market.

Modern Quito

Parque La Alameda has the oldest **astronomical observatory** in South America dating to 1873. Refurbished in 2009, it is still operational and houses a museum ① *T257 0765, museum Tue-Sun 1000-1700, US$2, observations on clear nights Tue-Fri 1830-1930*. Just north of the observatory, there is an excellent free light and music show with water fountains Friday and Saturday from 1900-2100, dress warmly. There is also a splendid monument to Simón Bolívar, lakes, and in the northwest corner a spiral lookout tower with a good view. A short distance north of Parque La Alameda, opposite Parque El Ejido, at the junction 6 de Diciembre and Patria, there is a large cultural and museum complex housing the **Casa de la Cultura** ① *T222 3392, ext 320, Tue-Fri 1000-1800, Sat 1000-1400, US$2, good toilets*, and the Museo Nacional del Banco Central del Ecuador (see below). Museums belonging to the Casa de la Cultura are: **Museo de Arte Moderno**, paintings and sculpture since 1830; **Colección Etnográfica**, traditional dress and adornments of indigenous groups; **Museo de Instrumentos Musicales**, an impressive collection of musical instruments, said to be the second in importance in the world.

If you have time to visit only one museum in Quito, it should be the **Museo Nacional del Banco Central del Ecuador** ① *entrance on Patria, T222 3259, Tue-Fri 0900-1700, Sat-Sun 1000-1600, US$2, guided tours in English, French or German by appointment*, also housed in the Casa de la Cultura. Of its five sections, the **Sala de Arqueología** is particularly impressive with beautiful pre-Columbian ceramics. The **Sala de Oro** has a nice collection of prehispanic gold objects. The remaining three sections house art collections: the **Sala de Arte Colonial** (rich in paintings and sculptures especially of religious themes), the **Sala de Arte Republicano** and the **Sala de Arte Contemporáneo**. There are also temporary exhibits, videos on Ecuadorean culture, a bookshop and cafeteria. Near the Casa de la Cultura, in the Catholic University's cultural centre, is the **Museo Jijón y Caamaño** ① *12 de Octubre y Roca, T299 1700 ext 1242, Mon-Fri 0830-1300, 1400-1600, US$2*, with a private collection of archaeological objects, historical documents, art, portraits, uniforms, etc, very well displayed.

A focal point in La Mariscal, north of Parque El Ejido, is **Plaza del Quinde**, also called **Plaza Foch** (Reina Victoria y Foch), a popular meeting place surrounded by cafés and restaurants. At the corner of Reina Victoria and La Niña is the excellent **Museo Mindalae** ① *T223 0609, www.sinchisacha.org, Mon-Sat 0930-1730, Sun 1030-1630, US$3, first Sun of*

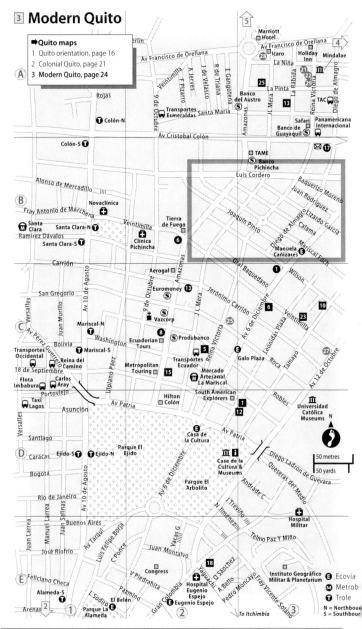

3 Modern Quito

➡Quito maps
1 Quito orientation, page 16
2 Colonial Quito, page 21
3 Modern Quito, page 24

A

Av Francisco de Orellana
Berlín
Rojas
Veintimilla
F Barreto
J Jerves
R de Triana
E de Velasco
E Gangotena
9 de Octubre
Transportes Esmeraldas
Santa María
Av Cristóbal Colón
Marriott Hotel
Av Francisco de Orellana
Icaro
La Niña
La Pinta
La Rábida
Mindalae
Holiday Inn
Banco del Austro
L Mera
Amazonas
La Casa
Reina Victoria
TAC
25
13
Safari
Banco de Guayaquil
Panamericana Internacional
Colón-N
Colón-S

B
Alonso de Mercadillo
Fray Antonio de Marchena
Santa Clara
Ramírez Dávalos
Santa Clara-N
Santa Clara-S
Novaclinica
Veintimilla
Clínica Pichincha
Tierra de Fuego
6
TAME
Banco Pichincha
Luis Cordero
Joaquín Pinto
Baquerizo Moreno
Juan Rodríguez
Lizardo García
Diego de Almagro
Mariscal Foch
Manuela Cañizares
Wilson
Gral Baquedano
Catama

C
San Gregorio
Carrión
Av Pérez Guerrero
Juan Murillo
Av 10 de Agosto
Mariscal-N
Bolívia
Washington
Mariscal-S
Transportes Occidental
Reina del Camino
18 de Septiembre
Flota Imbabura
Carlos Aray
Taxi Lagos
Portoviejo
Asunción
Ulpiano Páez
Av Patria
Aerogal
Euromoney
13
Vazcorp
8
Ecuadorian Tours
Produbanco
5
Transportes Ecuador
Metropolitan Touring
15
Mercado Artesanal La Mariscal
Hilton Colón
South American Explorers
1
12
Amazonas
9 de Octubre
L Mera
Reina Victoria
Jerónimo Carrión
Av 6 de Diciembre
Leonidas Plaza
Galo Plaza
Roca
Tamayo
Veintimilla
6
10
23
27
Av 12 de Octubre
Robles
Universidad Católica Museums

D
Santiago
Caracas
Bogotá
Río de Janeiro
Ejido-S
Ejido-N
Parque El Ejido
Av 10 de Agosto
Av 6 de Diciembre
Casa de la Cultura
Casa de la Cultura & Museums
Parque El Arbolito
Av Patria
Diego Ladrón de Guevara
Queseras del Medio
Andrade C
Hospital Militar
50 metres
50 yards
N

E
Juan Larrea
Manuel Larrea
Juan Salinas
Feliciano Checa
Alameda-S
Arenas
2
1
Parque La Alameda
José Riofrío
Av Felipe Borja
Luis Felipe Borja
C Ponce
V Piedrahíta
Pazmiño
El Belén
L Sodiro
Gran Colombia
Juan Montalvo
Congress
18
Hospital Eugenio Espejo
Eugenio Espejo
Vargas G
Yaguachi
O Sánchez
A Bello
Pedro Moncayo
Fray Vicente Solano
Telmo Paz Y Miño
N Jimenez III
I Treviño III
Instituto Geográfico Militar & Planetarium
To Itchimbía
Ecovía
Metrobús
Trole
N = Northbound
S = Southbound

La Mariscal detail

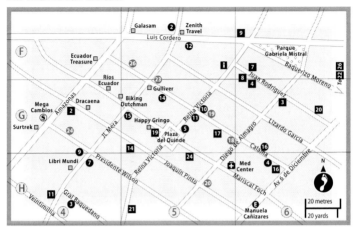

each month free, which exhibits Ecuadorean crafts and places them in their historical and cultural context, as well as temporary exhibits, a good fair-trade, non-profit shop and restaurant. (For another handicrafts museum and shop, see **Folklore**, page 37.)

North of La Mariscal is the large **Parque La Carolina**, a favourite recreational spot at weekends. Around it is the banking district, several shopping malls and hotels and restaurants. In the park is the **Jardín Botánico** ① T333 2516, daily 0900-1700 US$3.50, www.jardinbotanicoquito.com, which has a good cross section of Andean flora. Also the **Vivarium** ① T227 1799, Tue-Sun 0930-1730, US$3, dedicated to protect endangered snakes, reptiles and amphibians, and the **Museo de Ciencias Naturales** ① T244 9824, Mon-Fri 0830-1630, US$2.

Quito suburbs

East The **Santuario de Guápulo** ① *Mass Mon-Fri 1900, Sat 0700, Sun 0700-1200, 1600-1700* (1693, built by Indian slaves), perched on the edge of a ravine east of the city, is well worth seeing for its many paintings, gilded altars, stone carvings and the marvellously carved pulpit. The **Museo Fray Antonio Rodríguez** ① *Plaza de Guápulo N27-138, T256 5652, Mon-Thu 0900-1200, 1500-1730, Fri-Sat 0900-1200, US$1.50*, has religious art and furniture, from the 16th to the 20th centuries. Guided tours (Spanish only) include a visit to the beautiful Santuario.

Museo Guayasamín ① *Bosmediano 543, Bellavista, northeast of La Mariscal, T244 6445, Mon-Fri 1000-1700, US$3*, is highly recommended. Take a a taxi. As well as the eponymous artist's works there is a pre-Columbian and colonial collection. Works of art may be purchased (ask to see the whole collection) and also modern jewellery. Also presenting Guayasamín's work and 5 blocks from the museum is **La Capilla del Hombre** ① *Mariano Calvache y Lorenzo Chávez, Bellavista, T244 8492, www.capilladelhombre.com, Tue-Sun 1000-1730, US$3 (US$1 discount if visiting both sites)*, a collection of murals depicting the fate of Latin America from pre-Columbian to modern times.

In the eastern suburb of San Rafael is **La Casa de Kingman Museo** ① *Portoviejo 111 y Dávila, 1 block from San Rafael park, Valle de los Chillos, T286 1065, www.fundacion kingman.com, Thu-Sun 1000-1600, US$3*. This is a collection of the renowned artist's work and other colonial, republican and 20th-century art. Take a taxi or a Vingala bus from Isabel La Católica y Mena Caamaño, behind Universidad Católica.

West For spectacular views ride the **Teleférico** ① *Av Occidental above La Gasca, T222 1320, www.telefericoquito.com, daily 0800-2000, US$8 express (tourists may not use the US$4.50 regular service), children US$6, seniors US$4, service vans pick up at Trole terminals Norte and Recreo, and shopping malls Quicentro, El Jardín, CCI, no fixed schedule, more frequent at weekends, also from big hotels, Swiss, Hilton, Marriott and others for groups, US$1 each way*. The cable car is part of a complex with an amusement park, shops and food courts. It climbs to 4050 m on the flanks of Pichincha, where there are walking trails, including one to the summit of Rucu Pichincha, and horse riding just past the fence, see page 39.

Parque Arqueológico y Ecológico Rumipamba ① *east side of Av Occidental just north of Mariana de Jesús, T295 7576, www.fonsal.gov.ec, Wed-Sun 0800-1630, free, some English speaking guides*, is a 32-ha park on the slopes of Pichincha, where vestiges of human occupation of several pre-Inca periods, dating from 1500 BC to AD 1500, have been found. Excavated strata show the different ages, with debris from Pichincha's 1660 eruption being the most recent. On one site, several superimposed dwellings separated by mud flows can be seen. There are stone walls, circular mud dwellings, burials of different periods, grindstones and ceramics. The Quitus (AD 500-1500) farmed the area and traded with coast and Amazon until the invasion of the Incas. In 2010, the site continues to be studied. Pastures cover most of the grounds, in a few forested pockets, 36 native species of plants including three endemics have been identified. There are some walking trails including a *culunco*, a path in a gully surrounded by vegetation, characteristic of the Yumbo trade routes which linked Quito with the lowlands to the west.

Northwest of Rumipamba, in the neighbourhood of San Vicente de la Florida, is **Museo de Sitio La Florida** ① *C Antonio Costas y Román, T258 4962, www.fonsal.gov.ec, Wed-Sun*

0800-1630, free, some English-speaking guides. At this necropolis of the Quitus people, ten 17-m-deep burial chambers, dating to AD 220-640, have been excavated. The elaborate dress found in the tombs suggests most were prominent citizens; for example one body was dressed in fine cotton, highly decorated, topped with poncho adorned with 50 pieces of gold, 50 of copper and semi-precious stones. A less important person was just buried inside a sack. The women measured 1.55 m, the men 1.60-1.65 m. Their faces had aquiline features, not the wide nostrils or prominent cheek bones associated normally with Andean peoples. Burials also included ceramics, garments decorated with spondylus and mother of pearl shells, and gold.

Mitad del Mundo and around

The location of the equatorial line here (23 km north of central Quito, the suburbs stretch almost to the monument) was determined by Charles-Marie de la Condamine and his French expedition in 1736, and agrees to within 150 m with modern GPS measurements. The monument forms the focal point of a park and leisure area built as a typical colonial town, with restaurants, gift shops, post office with philatelic sales, travel agency, and has a very interesting **ethnographic museum** inside ① *Mon-Thu 0900-1800, Fri-Sun 0900-1900 (very crowded on Sun), US$2, children US$1, includes entrance to the pavilions; entry to the ethnographic museum US$3 (includes guided tour of museum in Spanish or English).* In the museum, a lift takes you to the top, then you walk down with the museum laid out all around with different indigenous cultures every few steps. There is a **Planetarium** ① *US$1.50, group of 15 minimum*, with hourly 30-minute shows and an attractive and interesting **model of old Quito**, about 10 sq m, with artificial day and night, which took seven years to build. **Museo Inti-Ñan** ① *200 m north of the monument, T239 5122, www.museointinan.com.ec, daily 0930-1730, US$3*, eclectic, very interesting and lots of fun activities, gives Equator certificates for visitors. Research about the equator and its importance to prehistoric cultures is carried out near Cayambe, by an organization called **Quitsa-to** ① *www.quitsato.org.*

Quito listings

For Sleeping and Eating price codes and other relevant information, see pages 10-11.

⌂ Sleeping

www.hotelesquito.com lists some high-end establishments. There are no good places to stay near the airport. A few simple places have opened near the Quitumbe bus terminal and there is one simple hostal (**$** Madrid) is opposite the Carcelén bus terminal, along busy Avenida Eloy Alfaro. Plan ahead about what type of lodgings and what part of town best suit you, and take a cab to your first choice. Large international chain hotels are represented in the city and meet their international standards.

Colonial Quito *p20, map p21*
$$$$ Mansión del Angel, Los Ríos N13-134 y Pasaje Gándara, T254 0293, www.mansiondelangel.com.ec. Luxurious hotel decorated with antiques in a beautifully renovated mansion, 15 ample rooms and a palacial suite, includes breakfast, dinner available, Wi-Fi, nice gardens, lovely atmosphere.
$$$$ Patio Andaluz, García Moreno N6-52 y Olmedo, T228 0830,

www.hotelpatioandaluz. com. 5-star
boutique hotel in the heart of the colonial
city, beautifully reconstructed 16th-century
mansion with large arches, balconies and
patios, exclusive restaurant with Ecuadorean
and Spanish cuisine, 22 rooms, library,
Folklore Olga Fisch gift shop.

$$$$ Plaza Grande, García Moreno N5-16,
Plaza de la Indpendencia, T251 0777,
www.plaza grandequito.com. Exclusive
top-of-the-line hotel with an exceptional
location, 15 suites including a presidential
suite for US$2000, 3 restaurants including **La
Belle Epoque**, gourmet French cuisine and a
wine cellar, jacuzzi in all rooms, climate
control, mini-spa, 110/220V outlets.

$$$$ Relicario del Carmen, Venezuela
1041 y Olmedo, T228 9120,
www.hotelrelicariodel carmen.com.
Beautifully refurbished colonial house,
includes breakfast, good restaurant, cafeteria,
Wi-Fi, good rooms and service, no smoking.

$$$$ Villa Colonna, Benalcázar 11-28 y
Esmeraldas, T295 5805, www.villacolonna.ec.
Exclusive boutique bed and breakfast with 6
elegant suites, includes breakfast in elegant
kitchen/dining room, personalized attention
from the owners who live here, no smoking.

$$$ Catedral Internacional, Mejía Oe6-36
y Cuenca, T295 5438. Nicely restored colonial
house with 15 carpeted rooms, small patio
with fountain, includes breakfast, popular
restaurant, heaters, spa, Wi-Fi, under new
management and completely refurbished in
2009.

$$$ Posada Colonial, García Moreno 1160 y
Mejía, T228 0282. Nicely refurbished colonial
house in a good location, includes breakfast,
restaurant serves economical set meals,
electric shower, Wi-Fi, a bit pricey.

$$$ San Francisco de Quito, Sucre Oe3-17 y
Guayaquil, T295 1241. Converted colonial
building, includes breakfast in attractive patio or
underground cloisters, restaurant, sauna, jacuzzi,
Wi-Fi, suites are particularly good value, well run
by owners, rooms to the street can be noisy.

$$$ Viena Internacional, Flores 600 y Chile,
T295 9611. Nice rooms and courtyard, good
restaurant (0700-1900).

$ Benalcázar, Benalcázar N1-88 y Bolívar,
Plaza de San Francisco, T295 8302, hotelbenal
cazar@hotmail.com. Refurbished colonial
house, cheaper with shared bath, hot water,
clean basic rooms, good value and location.

$ Chicago, Los Ríos N17-30 y Briceño, T228
1695. Popular family-run hostel, small rooms,
includes breakfast, cheaper in dorm, hot
water, Wi-Fi, internet in sitting room, laundry
and cooking facilities, a good economy
option.

$ Flores, Flores N3-51 y Sucre, T228 0435,
www.hotelflores.com.ec. Nicely refurbished
and decorated, private bath, hot water,
laundry facilities, patio, good value.

$ Huasi Continental, Flores N3-08 y Sucre,
T295 7327. Colonial house, restaurant,
cheaper with shared bath, hot water, Wi-Fi,
parking, good value.

$ Margarita 2, Los Ríos N12-108 y Espinoza,
T295 0441, www.hostalmargarita2.com.
Private bath, hot water, Wi-Fi downstairs,
good beds, sheets changed daily, good value.
Recommended.

$ The Guest House, Julio Castro E6-16 y
Valparaíso, no sign, T252 5834, www.quito-
guest-house.com. Nicely restored house,
rooms with bath for long stays, hot water,
Wi-Fi, laundry and cooking facilities, nice
views, discounts in low season, helpful, tour
operator, US$220/month/couple.

Modern Quito *p23, map p24*

$$$$ Café Cultura, Robles E6-62, relocating
to Washington y Páez in late 2011, T250 4078,
www.cafecultura.com. A well-established
hotel relocating to a renovated early 1900s
mansion (www.cafecultura.com/
new_project) with ample suites, social areas
including wood-paneled library with
fireplace, restaurant, attentive service.

$$$$ Le Parc, República de El Salvador
N34-349 e Irlanda, T227 6800,

www.leparc.com.ec. Modern hotel with 30 executive suites, full luxury facilities and service, includes buffet breakfast, restaurant, spa, gym, includes airport transfers.

$$$$ Nü House, Foch E6-12 y Reina Victoria, T255 7845, www.nuhousehotels.com. Modern luxury hotel with minimalist decor, includes breakfast, restaurant, some suites with jacuzzi, plug-in internet, all furnishings and works of art are available for sale.

$$$ Casa Helbling, Veintimilla E8-152 y 6 de Diciembre, T222 6013, www.casahelbling.de. Very good, popular hostel, spotless, breakfast available, cheaper with shared bath, Wi-Fi, laundry and cooking facilities, English, French and German spoken, family atmosphere, good information, tours arranged, luggage storage, help for motorcyclists, parking. Highly recommended.

$$$ Cayman, Rodríguez E7-29 y Reina Victoria, T256 7616, www.hotelcaymanquito.com. Pleasant hotel, includes breakfast in lovely bright dining room, cafeteria, Wi-Fi, parking, rooms a bit small, sitting room with fireplace, garden, very good.

$$$ Finlandia, Finlandia N32-129 y Suecia, T224 4288, www.hotelfinlandia.com.ec. Pleasant small hostel in residential area, buffet breakfast, restaurant, Wi-Fi, parking, spacious rooms, sitting room with fireplace, small garden, airport pickup extra, helpful staff.

$$$ El Arupo, Juan Rodríguez E7-22 y Reina Victoria, T255 7543, www.hostalelarupo.com. Good hostel, includes breakfast, Wi-Fi, laundry and cooking facilities, English and French spoken. Recommended.

$$$ Fuente de Piedra I & II, Wilson E9-80 y Tamayo and JL Mera N23-21 y Baquedano, T290 0323, www.ecuahotel.com. Nicely decorated modern hotels, comfortable, includes breakfast, Wi-Fi, some rooms are small, nice sitting areas, pleasant.

$$$ G House, Plaza 170 y 18 de Septiembre, T252 3577, www.hotelacartuja.com.

(Formerly **La Cartuja**). In the former British Embassy, includes breakfast, cafeteria, Wi-Fi, parking, beautifully decorated, spacious comfortable rooms, lovely garden, very helpful and hospitable. Highly recommended.

$$$ Hostal de la Rábida, La Rábida 227 y Santa María, T222 2169, www.hostalrabida.com. Lovely converted home, bright comfortable rooms, good restaurant, Wi-Fi, parking, British/Italian-run. Recommended.

$$$ Hostelling International, Pinto E6-12 y Reina Victoria, T254 3995, hostellingquito@gmail.com. Pricey modern hostel with capacity for 75, includes breakfast, cafeteria, Wi-Fi, coin-operated laundry, a variety of simple rooms from double with private bath to dorms (**$** per person), discounts for IYHF members.

$$$ Hothello, Amazonas N20-20 y 18 de Septiembre, T256 5835. Small modern hotel, bright and tastefully decorated rooms, includes nice breakfast, Wi-Fi in café, heating, helpful multilingual staff.

$$$ La Casa Sol, Calama 127 y 6 de Diciembre, T223 0798, www.lacasasol.com. Small hotel with courtyard, includes breakfast, 24-hr cafeteria, Wi-Fi downstairs, very helpful, English and French spoken, also run **Casa Sol** in Otavalo. Recommended.

$$$ Posada del Maple, Rodríguez E8-49 y 6 de Diciembre, T254 4507, www.posadadelmaple.com. Popular hostel, includes breakfast, cheaper with shared bath and in dorm, cooking facilities, warm atmosphere, free tea and coffee.

$$$ Rincón Escandinavo, Plaza N24-306 y Baquerizo Moreno, T222 5965, www.hotelescandinavo.com. Small well-furnished modern hotel, includes breakfast, restaurant, Wi-Fi, English spoken.

$$$ Sierra Madre, Veintimilla E9-33 y Tamayo, T250 5687, www.hotelsierramadre.com. Fully renovated old-style villa, restaurant, Wi-Fi, parking, nice sun roof, comfortable.

$$$ Sol de Quito, Alemania N30-170 y Vancouver, T254 1773, www.soldequito.com. Lovely converted home with large sitting room and library decorated with antiques, includes breakfast, restaurant, Wi-Fi, parking, comfortable rooms, suites have beautiful carved doors. Recommended.

$$$ Travellers Inn, La Pinta E4-435 y Amazonas, T255 6985, www.travellersecuador.com. In a nicely converted home, includes good breakfast, other meals on request, cheaper with shared bath, parking, pleasant common area, bike rentals.

$$$ Villa Nancy, Muros N27-94 y 12 de Octubre, T256 2483, www.hotelvillanancy.com. Quaint hotel in quiet residential area, includes buffet breakfast, Wi-Fi, parking, airport transfers extra, homey and comfortable, helpful multilingual staff. Recommended.

$ Amazonas Inn, Pinto E4-324 y Amazonas, T222 5723, www.amazonasinn.com. Very nice, hot water, café, Wi-Fi, carpeted rooms, some are noisy, 1st floor best, spotless. Recommended.

$ Backpackers Inn, Rodríguez E7-48 y Reina Victoria, T250 9669, www.backpackersinn.net. Popular hostel, breakfast available, cheaper with shared bath or in dorm (**$**), hot water, Wi-Fi, laundry and cooking facilities, adequate dorms.

$ Casona de Mario, Andalucía 213 y Galicia (La Floresta), T254 4036, www.casonademario.com. Popular hostel, shared bath, hot water, laundry facilities, well equipped kitchen, parking, sitting room, nice garden, book exchange, long stay discounts, Argentine owner. Repeatedly recommended.

$ El Cafecito, Cordero E6-43 y Reina Victoria, T223 4862, www.cafecito.net. Popular with backpackers, good café including vegetarian, cheaper in dorm (**$**), 1 room with bath, hot water, relaxed atmosphere but can get noisy at night, Canadian-owned.

$ L'Auberge Inn, Colombia N15-200 y Yaguachi, T255 2912, www.auberge-inn-hostal.com. Nice spacious rooms, duvets on beds, cheaper with shared bath, excellent hot water, restaurant, spa, Wi-Fi, cooking facilities, parking, lovely garden, terrace and communal area, tour operator, helpful, good atmosphere. Highly recommended.

$ La Galería, Calama 233 y Almagro, T250 0307, hostallagaleria@hotmail.com. Nice family-run hostel, private bath, hot water, internet in sitting-room, cooking facilities, carpeted rooms, patio with tables, English spoken.

$ Queen's Hostel/Hostal De La Reina, Reina Victoria N23-70 y Wilson, T255 1844, hostaldelareina@hotmail.com. Nice small hotel, popular among travellers and Ecuadoreans, cafeteria, private bath, hot water, Wi-Fi, cooking facilities, sitting room with fireplace. Recommended.

$ Secret Garden, Antepara E4-60 y Los Ríos, T295 6704, www.secretgardenquito.com. Restored old house, some rooms small and dark, lovely roof-top terrace restaurant for breakfast and dinner (vegetarian available), 4 rooms with private bath, cheaper in dorm, hot water, popular meeting and party place, can be noisy. Ecuadorean/Australian-owned, also run a rustic lodge between Pasochoa and Cotopaxi, www.secretgardencotopaxi.com.

$ Titisee, Foch E7-60 y Reina Victoria, T252 9063. Nice place, large rooms, cheaper with shared bath, hot water, internet, cooking facilities, lounge, book exchange, helpful owner. Recommended.

$ Villa Nancy, 6 de Diciembre N24-398 y Cordero, T256 3084, www.villa-nancy.com. Nice place, includes buffet breakfast, most rooms with private bath, hot water, Wi-Fi, cooking facilities, sitting room, terrace, airport pickup, travel information, Swiss/Ecuadorean-run, helpful.

Apartments

$$$ Antinea, Rodríguez 175 y Almagro, T250 6839, www.hotelantinea.com. Rooms, suites and apartments in nicely refurbished

house with a French touch, includes breakfast, heating, Wi-Fi, parking, tastefully decorated, from US$1160 per month, good service.
$$ Amaranta, Leonidas Plaza N20-32 y Washington, T254 3619, www.aparthotel amaranta.com. Includes breakfast, good restaurant, Wi-Fi in restaurant and some rooms, parking, comfortable, well-equipped suites, from US$950 per month.
$$ Apartamentos Modernos, Amazonas N31-181 y Mariana de Jesús, T223 3766 ext 800, www.apartamentosmodernos. com.ec. Convenient location near El Jardín Mall and Parque La Carolina, 1- and 2-bedroom flats from US$600 per month, Wi-Fi extra, parking, English and German spoken, good value.

Quito suburbs *p26*
$$$$ Hacienda Rumiloma, Obispo Díaz de La Madrid, final de la calle, T254 8206, www.haciendarumiloma.com. Luxurious hotel in a 40-ha hacienda on the slopes of Pichincha. Sumptuous suites, each one individually designed with lots of attention to detail, lounges decorated with antiques, includes breakfast, pricey restaurant offers good quality Ecuadorean and international cuisine, bar with fireplace, nice views, personalized attention from dynamic owners Amber and Oswaldo Freire, ideal for someone looking for a luxurious escape not far from the city.
$$$$ Hostería San Jorge, Km 4 via antigua Quito-Nono, to the west of Av Occidental, T339 0403, www.eco-lodgesanjorge.com. Converted 18th-century hacienda on a 80 ha private reserve on the slopes of Pichincha, includes breakfast, full board available, good pricey restaurant, heating, pool, sauna and jacuzzi, Wi-Fi in lounge, airport transfers, horse riding and birdwatching. Nature reserve (part of a group of reserves) has páramo and one of the few remnants of native forest near Quito. Recommended.

● **Eating**

Eating out in Quito is excellent, varied, upmarket and increasingly cosmopolitan. In colonial Quito there are a number of elegant restaurants offering Ecuadorean and international food. Small simple places serving set meals for US$2-4 are everywhere; most close by early evening and on Sun.

Colonial Quito *p20, map p21*
$$$ El Ventanal, Carchi y Nicaragua, west of the Basílica, in Parque San Juan, take a taxi to the parking area and a staff member will accompany you along a footpath to the restaurant, T257 2232, www.elventanal.ec. Tue-Sat 1200-1500, 1800-2200, Sun 1200-1700. International nouvelle cuisine with a varied menu including a number of seafood dishes, fantastic views over the city.
$$$ Mea Culpa, Palacio Arzobispal, Plaza de la Independencia, T295 1190, www.meaculpa. com.ec. Mon-Fri 1215-1530, 1900-2300, Sat 1900-2300. Formal and elegant (dress code), international and Mediterranean gourmet food, reservations required.
$$$ Theatrum, Plaza del Teatro, 2nd floor of Teatro Sucre, T228 9669, www.theatrum. com.ec. Mon-Fri 1230-1600, 1930-2330, Sat-Sun 1900-2300. Excellent creative gourmet cuisine in the city's most important theatre, wide selection of fruit desserts which come with an explanatory card.
$$$-$$ Los Geranios, Morales Oe1-134, T228 3889. Daily 0900-0100. Upscale *comida típica*, in a nicely restored **La Ronda** house.
$$ Hasta la Vuelta Señor, Pasaje Arzobispal, 3rd floor. Mon-Sat 1100-2300, Sun 1100-2100. A *fonda quiteña* perched on an indoor balcony with Ecuadorean *comida típica* and snacks, try their *empanadas* (pasties) or a *seco de chivo* (goat stew).
$$ Tianguez, Plaza de San Francisco under the portico of the church. Mon-Tue 0930-1830, Wed-Sun 0930-2400. International and local dishes, good coffee,

snacks, sandwiches, popular, also craft shop (closes 1830), run by Fundación Sinchi Sacha.

$$-$ La Fuente del Conquistador, Benalcázar N7-44 y Olmedo. Mon-Sat 1200-1530. Economical set lunches, grill, local and international food à la carte.

$ Criollo, Flores N7-31 y Olmedo. Mon-Sat 0800-2130, Sun 0800-1700. Economical set meals (a bit pricier at weekends), tasty chicken dishes and Ecuadorean food à la carte.

$ Govinda, Esmeraldas Oe3-115 y Venezuela. Mon-Sat 0800-1600. Vegetarian dishes, good value economical set meals and à la carte, also breakfast.

Cafés

Café del Teatro, Plaza del Teatro opposite Teatro Sucre. Daily 1000-2100, open later when there are events at the theatres. Snacks, cakes, drinks and some meals, nice location and atmosphere.

Vista Hermosa, Mejía 453 y García Moreno. Mon-Sat 1400-0000, Sun 1200-2100. Drinks, pizza, light meals, live music on weekends, lovely terrace-top views of the colonial centre.

Modern Quito *p23, map p24*
$$$ Chez Jérôme, Whymper N30-96 y Coruña, T223 4067. Mon-Fri 1230-1530, 1930-2330, Sat 1930-2330. Excelent French cuisine, traditional and modern dishes with a touch of local ingredients, good ambiance and service.

$$$ La Choza, 12 de Octubre N24-551 y Cordero, T223 0839. Mon-Fri 1200-1600, 1800-2200, Sat-Sun 1200-1700. Traditional Ecuadorean cuisine, good music and decor.

$$$ La Gloria, Valladolid N24-519 y Salazar, La Floresta, T252 7855. Daily 1200-1530, 1900-2200. Very innovative Peruvian and international cuisine, excellent food and service, same ownership as Theatrum.

$$$ La Jaiba, Coruña y San Ignacio, T254 3887. Daily 1100-1600, Tue-Sat also

1900-2130. An old favourite for seafood, good service.

$$$ La Viña, Isabel la Católica y Cordero, T256 6033. Mon-Fri 1230-1500, 1930-2300, Sat 1930-2300. Classy restaurant with an extensive and unusual menu, many French and Italian dishes, very good food, presentation, comfort and service, top of the line.

$$$ Los Troncos, Los Shyris N35-80 y Portugal, T243 7377, Mon-Sat 1230-2200, Sun 1230-1600. Good Argentine grill, serves meats, fish, pasta, salads, small and friendly, busy on Sun.

$$$ Rincón de La Ronda, Bello Horizonte 406 y Almagro, T254 0459, www.rinconlaronda. com. Daily 1200-2300. Very good local and international food, huge Sun buffet, sun night folklore show, gets many tour groups. Touristy.

$$$ Sake, Paul Rivet N30-166 y Whymper, T252 4818, www.sakerestaurants.com. Mon-Sat 1230-1530, 1830-2300, Sun 12305-1600, 1830-2200. Sushi bar and other Japanese dishes, very trendy, great food, nicely decorated.

$$$ Zazu, Mariano Aguilera 331 y La Pradera, T254 3559, www.zazuquito.com. Mon-Fri 1230-1500, 1900-2230, Sat 1900-2230. Very elegant and exclusive dining. International and Peruvian specialities, extensive wine list, attentive service, reservations required.

$$$-$$ La Briciola, Toledo 1255 y Salazar, T254 7138. Daily 1200-2400. Extensive Italian menu, excellent food, homey atmosphere, very good personal service.

¶¶ Coffee & Toffee, Calama E8-28 y Almagro, open 24 hrs. Very good international food, breakfasts, coffee and snacks, generous portions, pleasant atmosphere, Wi-Fi.

$$ Il Risotto, Eloy Alfaro N34-447 y Portugal. Sun-Fri 1200-1500, 1800-2300. Very popular and very good italian cooking, live music Thu and Fri. A Quito tradition.

$$ La Boca del Lobo, Calama 284 y Reina Victoria. Sun-Wed 1700-2330, Thu-Sat

1700-0030, bar closes 1 hr later. Stylish bar-restaurant with eclectic food, drink, decor, and atmosphere, good food and cocktails, popular, good meeting place.

$$ Mama Clorinda, Reina Victoria N24-150 y Calama. Daily 1100-2300. Ecuadorean cuisine à la carte and set meals, filling, good value.

$$ Paléo, Cordero E5-36 y JL Mera. Mon-Sat 1200-1500 1830-2200. Authentic Swiss specialities such as rösti and raclette. Also good economical set lunch, pleasant ambiance. Recommended.

$$ Pekín, Whymper N26-42 y Orellana. Mon-Sat 1200-1500, 1900-2230, Sun 1200-2030. Excellent Chinese food, very nice atmosphere.

$$ Sushi/Siam, Calama E5-104 y JL Mera. Mon-Sat 1200-2300, Sun 1200-1600. Sushi bar, small portions, pleasant atmosphere with nice balcony, good value happy hour 1700-1900.

$$ The Magic Bean, Foch E5-08 y JL Meral. Daily 0700-2200. Specializes in fine coffees and natural foods, more than 20 varieties of pancakes, good salads, large portions, outdoor seating (also offers popular lodging, **$**).

$$-$ Baalbek, 6 de Diciembre N23-123 y Wilson. Daily 1200-1800. Authentic Lebanese cuisine, great food and atmosphere, friendly service.

$$-$ El Hornero, Veintimilla y Amazonas, República de El Salvador y Los Shyris and on Gonzalez Suárez. Daily 1200-2300. Very good wood-oven pizzas, try one with *choclo* (fresh corn). Recommended.

$$-$ Las Palmeras, Japón N36-87 y Naciones Unidas, opposite Parque la Carolina and other locations. Daily 0800-1700. Very good *comida esmeraldeña*, try their hearty viche soup, outdoor tables, popular, good value. Recommended.

$$-$ Uncle Ho's, Calama E8-29 y Almagro. Mon-Sat 1200-2230. Good Asian cooking, especially a number of Vietnamese dishes, set meals for lunch and à la carte, cocktails, Wi-Fi, popular.

$ Chandani Tandoori, JL Mera 1312 y Cordero. Mon-Sat 1100-2200. Good authentic Indian cuisine, economical set meals, popular, good value. Recommended.

$ Chez Alain, Baquedano E5-26 y JL Mera. Mon-Fri 1200-1530. Choice of good 4-course set lunches, US$5, pleasant relaxed atmosphere. Recommended.

$ Sakti, Carrión E4-144 y Amazonas. Mon-Fri 0830-1830. Good-quality and value vegetarian food, breakfast, set lunches and à la carte, fruit juices, great desserts, (also a few hostel rooms at the back, **$**).

$ Yu Su, Almagro y Colón, edif Torres de Almagro. Mon-Fri 1230-1600, 1800-2000, Sat 1230-1600. Very good sushi bar, pleasant, Korean-run, takeaway service.

Cafés

Coffee Tree, Reina Victoria y Foch, Plaza del Quinde, also at Plaza de los Presidentes and Museo Mindalae (La Niña y Reina Victoria). Open 24 hrs. Popular cafés serving a variety of snacks, pasta, burguers, coffee, Wi-Fi .

Este Café, JL Mera N23-94 y Baquedano, Mon-Sat 0800-2400, Sun 0900-1800, also at Amazonas N32-135 y La Granja, Mon-Sat 0730-2230. Popular cafés, good organic coffee and sweets, healthy snacks, set lunches and salad bar on weekdays, cocktails, also have live music and other cultural events.

Ethnic Coffee, Amazonas N21-81 y Robles. Mon-Sat 0800-2000. Nice café in one of the **Ethnic Collection** craft shops, offers gourmet coffee as well as a wide range of desserts, meals and drinks.

Kallari, Wilson y JL Mera, www.kallari.com. Mon-Fri 0800-1830, Sat 0900-1830. Fair-trade café, breakfast, snacks, salad and sandwich set lunches, organic coffee and chocolate, crafts, run by an association of farmers and artisans from the Province of Napo working on rainforest and cultural conservation. Repeatedly recommended.

Mirador de Guápulo, Rafael León Larrea, behind **Hotel Quito**. Tue-Sat 1600-0000 or later. Snacks such as *empanadas*, crêpes, sandwiches, drinks, live music Thu-Sat from 2130, great views, portable heaters for outdoor seating at night.

🔊 Bars and clubs

Note that a law introduced in 2010 forbids the sale and consumption of alcohol on Sun.

New City *p23, map p24*

Bungalow Six, Almagro N24-139 y Calama, T09-520 8955. Tue-Sat 1900-0200, Sun 1200-1900. US-style sports bar and club. Popular place to hang out and watch a game or a film, dancing later on, varied music, cover US$5 (Thu free), ladies' night on Wed, happy hour 2000-2200.

El Aguijón, Calama E7-35 y Reina Victoria, T256 9014. Tue-Sat 2100-0300. Bohemian bar/club, varied music, nice atmosphere, after 2200 entry US$6 with 1 free drink. Also concerts, theatre, art.

El Pobre Diablo, Isabel La Católica y Galicia E12-06 , La Floresta, T222 5194. Mon-Sat 1230-0200. Relaxed atmosphere, friendly, jazz, sandwiches, snacks and nice meals, live music Wed, Thu and Sat, a popular place to hang out and chill.

Finn McCool's, Almagro N24-64 y Pinto, T252 1780. Daily 1100-0200. Irish-run pub, Irish and international food, darts, pool, table football, English football and other sports on TV, Wi-Fi, popular meeting place.

Flash Back, González Suárez N27-205 y Muros, T322 6922. Opposite **Hotel Quito**. Club, mostly English music, rock and 1980s music, older crowd, cover US$12.

Ghoz, La Niña E6-62 y Reina Victoria, T255 6255. Tue-Sat 1800-0200. Swiss food, pool, darts, videos, games, music.

Kings Cross, Reina Victoria N26-155 y La Niña, T09-972 3379. Mon-Fri 1730-0200, Sat 1830-0100. Classic rock, BBQ, best hamburgers, wings. Popular with all ages. Recommended.

La Juliana, 12 de Octubre N24-722 y Coruña,

T604 1569. Thu-Sat 2130-0300. Popular club, live 1990s Latin music, cover US$12.

Mario's, Roca E4-115 y Amazonas, at Hotel Windsor, T222 4033. Mon-Sat 1600-0100. Elegant place to relax, listen to classical music and enjoy tropical drinks, older crowd.

No Bar, Calama E5-01 y JL Mera. Mon-Sat 1900-0300, good mix of Latin and Euro dance music, busy at weekends. Free drinks for women until 2200, Thu-Sat after 2200 entry US$5 with 1 free drink.

Patatu's, Wilson 758 y JL Mera, T250 5233. Mon-Sat 1900-0200. Good drinks, pool table, happy hour all night Mon, loud music, dancing, owner speaks English and German.

Ramón Antiguo, Mena Caamaño e Isabel la Católica, 2100-0200. Live music Fri-Sat, cover US$5-10 depending on band. Great for salsa and other hip tropical music, popular with locals.

Reina Victoria Pub, Reina Victoria 530 y Roca, T222 6369. Mon-Sat 1700-2400. Relaxed English-style pub, good selection of microbrews and of Scottish and Irish whiskys, moderately priced bar meals, darts, popular meeting point for British and US expats.

Santurrón, Calama E4-363 y Amazonas, T254 9684. Tue-Sat 1800-0300. Classy, a good place to hang out, listen to music (live some nights) and dance, no entry fee, happy hour 1800-2100.

Seseribó, Veintimilla 325 y 12 de Octubre, T256 3598. Thu-Sat 2100-0100. Caribbean music and salsa, a must for salseros, very popular, especially Thu and Fri, cover US$8. Recommended.

Turtle's Head, La Niña 626 y JL Mera, T256 5544. Mon-Tue 1700-0300, Wed-Sat 1230-0300. Microbrews, fish and chips, curry, pool table, darts, fun atmosphere.

Varadero, Reina Victoria N26-99 y La Pinta, T254 2575. Mon-Thu1200-2400, Fri-Sat 1800-0300. Bar-restaurant, live Cuban music Wed-Sat, meals, snacks, good cocktails, older crowd and couples.

Quito *p17, maps p16, p21 and p24*
There are always many cultural events taking place in Quito, usually free of charge. For events at **Casa de la Cultura**, see http://cce.org.ec. Films are listed daily in *El Comercio*, www.elcomercio.com.

Cinema
Casa de la Cultura, Patria y 6 de Diciembre, T290 2272. Shows foreign films, often has documentaries, film festivals.
Ocho y Medio, Valladolid N24-353 y Guipuzcoa, La Floresta, T290 4720. Cinema and café, good for art films, programme available at *Libri Mundi* and elsewhere. There are several multiplexes, eg **Cinemark**, www.cinemark.com.ec, **Multicines**, www.multicines.com.ec, and **Supercines**. www.supercines.com.

Dance schools
One-to-one or group lessons are offered for US$4-6 per hr.
Son Latino, Reina Victoria N24-211 y García, T223 4340, several varieties of salsa.
Salsa y Merengue School, Foch E4-256 y Amazonas, T222 0427, also cumbia.
Universal Salsa, García E5-45 y JL Mera, T09-631 7757, salsa, capoeira and other dances.

Music
Folk Free folk shows at Palacio Arzobispal (entrance on C Venezuela), Fri at 1930, Sat at 1830 and Sun at 1130. The municipal brass band performs at Plaza del Teatro several mornings per week at 0900. Local folk music is popular in *peñas*; most places do not come alive until 2230:
Noches de Quito, Washington E5-29 y JL Mera, T223 4855. Thu-Sat 2000-0300, show starts 2130, varied music, entry US$6.
Ñucanchi, Av Universitaria Oe5-188 y Armero. T254 0967. Thu-Sat 2000-0300, show starts at 2130, Ecuadorean and other music,

including Latin dance later in the night, entry US$8-10.
Ecuadorean folk ballet: Ballet Andino Humanizarte, at Teatro Humanizarte, Plaza N24-226 y Baquerizo Moreno, T222 6116, www.humanizarte.com, Wed at 1930, US$10; plays and comedies are also often in their repertoire, restaurant on the premises.
Jacchigua, at **Teatro Demetrio Aguilera Malta**, Casa de la Cultura, 6 de Diciembre y Patria, T295 2025, www.jacchiguaesecuador.com, Wed at 1930; entertaining, colourful and touristy, reserve ahead, US$25. **Saruymanda**, at Palacio Arzobispal, Plaza de la Independencia, T273 5449, www.saruymanda.blogspot.com, Fri 1930, donations appreciated.
Classical the **Orquesta Sinfónica Nacional**, T250 2815, performs at **Teatro Sucre**, **Casa de la Música**, in the colonial churches and regionally. **Casa de la Música**, Valderrama s/n y Mariana de Jesús, T226 7093, www.casadelamusica.ec, concerts by the Orquesta Sinfónica Nacional, Orquesta Filarmónica del Ecuador, Orquesta de Instrumentos Andinos and invited performers. Excellent acoustics.

Theatre
Many old theatres have been restored by the municipality.
Agora, open-air theatre of Casa de la Cultura, 12 de Octubre y Patria. Stages plays, concerts.
Teatro Bolívar, Espejo 847 y Guayaquil, T258 2486, www.teatrobolivar.org. Despite restoration work there are tours, presentations and festivals.
Teatro Sucre, Plaza del Teatro, Manabí N8-131 y Guayaquil, T295 1661, www.teatrosucre.com. Beautifully restored 19th-century building, the city's main theatre.

Quito *p17, maps p16, p21 and p24*
New Year, Años Viejos: life-size puppets satirize politicians and others. At midnight on

31 Dec a will is read, the legacy of the outgoing year, and the puppets are burnt; good along Amazonas between Patria and Colón, very entertaining and good humoured. On New Year's day everything is shut. **6 Jan** (may be moved to the weekend), colourful **Inocentes** procesion from Plaza de Santo Domingo at 1700. **Palm Sunday**, colourful procession from the Basílica, 0800-1000. The solemn **Good Friday** processions are most impressive. **24 May** is **Independence**, commemorating the Battle of Pichincha in 1822 with early morning cannon-fire and parades, everything closes. **Aug**: Agosto Arte y Cultura, organized by the municipality, cultural events, dance and music in different places throughout the city. The city's main festival, **Día de Quito**, celebrated **1-6 Dec**, commemorates the foundation of the city with elaborate parades, bullfights, performances and music in the streets, very lively. Hotels charge extra, everything except a few restaurants shuts on 6 Dec. Foremost among **Christmas** celebrations is the **Misa del Gallo**, midnight Mass. Nativity scenes can be admired in many public places. Over Christmas, Quito is crowded, hotels are full and the streets are packed with vendors and shoppers.

⊙ Shopping

Quito p17, maps p16, p21 and p24
Shops open generally 0900-1900 on weekdays, some close at midday and most shut Sat afternoon and Sun. Shopping centres are open at weekends. The main shopping districts are along Av Amazonas in the north and C Guayaquil in the colonial city. In modern Quito much of the shopping is done in malls (see list under Foodstuffs).

Bookshops
Abya-Yala, 12 de Octubre 14-30 y Wilson. Good for books about indigenous cultures and anthropology, also has excellent library and museum.

Confederate Books, Calama 410 y JL Mera. Mon-Sat 1000-1800, excellent selection of second-hand books, including travel guides, mainly English but also German and French.
Damas Norteamericanas y Británicas Library, see page 47. Cheap second-hand English books.
Libri Mundi, JL Mera N23-83 y Veintimilla, Plaza del Quinde, Centro Cultural Metropolitano and Quicentro Shopping, www.librimundi.com. Excellent selection including English titles, sells Footprint guides, knowledgeable and helpful staff, noticeboard of what's on in Quito. Highly recommended.
Libro Express, Amazonas 816 y Veintimilla, also at Quicentro Shopping and airport. Has a good stock of maps, guides and international magazines.
Mr Books, Mall El Jardín, 3rd floor. Good stock, many in English including Footprint travel guides, open daily. Recommended.
The English Bookshop, Calama 217 y Almagro. Daily 1000-1800, good selection of second-hand books.

Camping
Camping gas is available many of the shops listed below, white gas (*combustible para lámpara Coleman, gasolina blanca*) at times from **Kywi**, Centro Comercial Olímpico, 6 de Diciembre, north of the stadium and 10 de Agosto N24-59. They also have rubber boots.
Los Alpes, Reina Victoria N23-45 y Baquedano. Local and imported equipment, also rentals.
Antisana, Centro Comercial El Bosque, ground floor. Local and imported, sales only.
Aventura Sport, Quicentro Shopping, top floor. Tents, good selection of glacier sunglasses, upmarket.
Camping Sports, Colón E6-39 y Reina Victoria. Sales only, well stocked.
Eko, Wilson y JL Mera. Kayaking supplies, ski jackets, fleeces.
Equipos Cotopaxi, 6 de Diciembre N20-36 y Patria. Ecuadorean and imported gear for sale.

Mono Dedo, JL Mera N23-84 y Wilson and Rafael León N24-36 y Coruña, www.monodedo.com. Climbing equipment, part of a rock climbing club.

Tatoo, JL Mera N23-54 y Wilson and CC La Esquina in Cumbayá, www.tatoo.ws. Quality backpacks and outdoor clothing.

The Altar, J L Mera N22-93 y Veintimilla. Imported and local gear for sale, good prices for rentals.

The Explorer, Reina Victoria y N24-43 Pinto. Sales and rentals, very helpful, will buy US or European equipment.

Foodstuffs

Galería Ecuador, Reina Victoria N24-263 y L García, T223 9469. Tue-Sun 1000-2200. Shop and café featuring Ecuadorean gourmet organic products (coffee, chocolate) and some crafts.

Mi Comisariato, a well-stocked supermarket and department store, at Quicentro Shopping (Naciones Unidas y Shyris) and García Moreno y Mejía in the colonial city.

Santa María, Av Iñaquito y Pereira, Bolívar 334 y Venezuela and Versalles y Carrión. Good value supermarkets.

Supermaxi at Mall El Jardín (Amazonas y República), CCI (Amazonas y Naciones Unidas), El Bosque (Occidental y Carvajal), Multicentro (6 de Diciembre y La Niña), Megamaxi (6 de Diciembre y Julio Moreno), and El Recreo. (Av Maldonado). Very well stocked supermarket and department store, local and imported goods.

Handicrafts

Note that there are controls on export of arts and crafts. Unless they are obviously new handicrafts, you may have to get a permit from the **Instituto Nacional de Patrimonio Cultural** (Colón Oe1-93 y 10 de Agosto, T254 3527, offices also in other cities), before you can mail or take things home. Permits cost US$6 and take time.

A wide selection can be found at the following craft markets: **Mercado**

Artesanal La Mariscal, Jorge Washington, between Reina Victoria and JL Mera, daily 1000-1800, interesting and worthwhile; **El Indio**, Roca E4-35 y Amazonas, daily 0900-1900; **Centro de Artesanías CEFA**, 12 de Octubre1738 y Madrid, Mon-Fri 0900-1900, Sat 0900-1700.

On weekends, crafts are sold in stalls at **Parque El Ejido** and along the Av Patria side of this park, artists sell their paintings (www.arte ejido.com). There are souvenir shops on García Moreno in front of the Palacio Presidencial in the colonial city. At the north end of the **Plaza de Santo Domingo** and along the nearest stretch of C Flores, local garments (for natives rather than tourists) can be seen and bought.

Recommended shops with an ample selection are:

Camari, Marchena 260 y Versalles. Fair Trade shop run by an artisan organization.

Folklore, Colón E10-53 y Caamaño, the store of the late Olga Fisch (died 1989), who came to Ecuador from Hungary in 1939 and who encouraged craftspeople to excel. Attractive selection of handicrafts and rugs, expensive but very good quality, open Mon-Fri 0900-1900, Sat 1000-1800; small museum upstairs, voluntary donations welcomed. Also at **Hotel Hilton Colón** and **Hotel Patio Andaluz**.

Galería Latina, JL Mera 823 y Veintimilla. Fine selection of alpaca and other handicrafts from Ecuador, Peru and Bolivia, visiting artists sometimes demonstrate their work.

Hilana, 6 de Diciembre N23-10 y Veintimilla Beautiful unique 100% wool blankets with Ecuadorean motifs, excellent quality, purchase by metre possible, reasonable prices.

Homero Ortega, Isabel La Católica N24-100 and Plaza San Francisco, facing the church. Outlet for Cuenca Panama hat manufacturer.

K Dorfzaun, at Quicentro mall, ground floor. Outlet for Cuenca Panama hat manufacturer.

Kallari, Crafts from Oriente at café, page 33.

La Bodega, JL Mera 614 y Carrión. Recommended for antiques and handicrafts.
Marcel Creations, Roca 766, entre Amazonas y 9 de Octubre. Panama hats.
Mindalae. Nice crafts at museum, page 23.
Productos Andinos, Urbina 111 y Cordero. Artisan's co-op, good selection, including unusual items.
Saucisa, Amazonas 2487 y Pinto, and a couple other locations in La Mariscal. Very good place to buy Andean music CDs and instruments.
The Ethnic Collection, Amazonas N21-81and N21-187 y Robles, www.ethniccollection.com. Wide variety of clothing, leather, bags, jewellery and ceramic items. Also café at N21-81.

Jewellery
Argentum, JL Mera 614. Excellent selection, reasonably priced.
Ari Gallery, Bolívar Oe6-23, Plaza de San Francisco, www.ushinajewellery.com, open daily. Fine silver with ancestral motifs.
Jeritsa, Mall El Jardín, local 234. Good selection, prices and service.
Taller Guayasamín, at the museum, see page 26. Jewellery with native designs.

Markets
Main produce markets, all accessible by Trole: **Mercado Central**, Av Pichincha y Olmedo (also on the Ecovía), **Mercado Santa Clara**, Versalles y Ramírez Dávalos and **Mercado Iñaquito**, Iñaquito y Villalengua.

▲ Activities and tours

Quito *p17, maps p16, p21 and p24*
Birdwatching and nature
The following operators specialize in birdwatching tours: **Andean Birding**, www.andeanbirding.com; **BirdEcuador**, www.birdecuador.com; **Neblina Forest**, www.neblinaforest.com; **Pluma Verde Tours**, www.plumaverdetours.com.

City tours
Paseos Culturales, at Plaza de la Independencia tourist information office, Venezuela y Espejo, T257 2445. Walking tours of the colonial city led by English-speaking officers of the Policía Metropolitana. Daily at 1000, 1100 and 1400, 2½-3 hrs, US$15, children and seniors US$7.50, includes museum entrance fees; Mon is not a good day because many museums are closed. Night tours require a minimum of 8 people, walking tours at 1800 and 1900, US$8; bus tours include El Panecillo and La Cima de la Libertad lookouts, US$20 pp, advance booking required.
Coches Victoria, horse-drawn carriages with an English-speaking guide will take you on a 20-min tour of the colonial heart. Tickets sold at booth on corner García Moreno y Sucre, T09-980 0723, Mon-Fri 1700-2300, Sat-Sun 1000-2300, US$4 pp, children and seniors US$2, reservations recommended at weekends.
Chiva Don Otto, tours of colonial Quito in a *chiva*, an old-fashioned open-sided bus. Sat and Mon-Thu. Contact **Klein Tours**, page 41.

Climbing and trekking
Climbs and trekking tours can be arranged in Quito and several other cities.. The following Quito operators specialize in this area, see Tour operators, below for their contact information: **Andes Explorer**, **Campo Base**, **Campus Trekking**, **Climbing Tours**, **Compañía de Guías**, **Cotopaxi Cara Sur**, **Ecuador Treasure**, **Gulliver**, **Latitud 0°**, **Palmar Voyages**, **Safari**, and **Sierra Nevada**.
   Note that independent guides do not normally provide a full service (ie transport, food, equipment, insurance) and, without a permit from the Ministerio del Ambiente, they may be refused entry to national parks, especially Cotopaxi. You must ensure that your operator, guide and transport have the requisite permits (*patentes*). A cheap tour may leave you stranded at the national park gates.

Cycling and mountain biking

Quito has a couple of bike paths including one around the perimeter of Parque La Carolina and another in the south, along Quebrada Ortega in the Quitumbe neighbourhood. The city organizes a *ciclopaseo*, a cycle day, every Sun 0900-1500. Key avenues are closed to vehicular traffic and thousands of cyclists cross the city in 29 km from north to south. This and other cycle events are run by **Fundación Ciclópolis**, Equinoccio N17 -171 y Queseras del Medio, T322 6502, www.ciclopolis.ec (in Spanish); they also hire bikes, US$5.60 per *ciclopaseo* (must book Mon-Fri), US$11.20 per day on other days. Rentals also from **La Casa del Ciclista** (see below), near the *ciclopaseo* route. **Biciacción**, www.biciaccion.org, has information about cycling routes in the city and organizes trips outside Quito.

Mountain-bike tours Many operators offer bike tours, the following are specialists: **Aries**, T09-981 6603, www.ariesbikecompany. com. 1- to 3-day tours, all equipment provided.
Biking Dutchman, Foch E 4-313 y JL Mera, T256 8323, after hours T09-420 5349, www.biking-dutchman.com. 1- and several-day tours, great fun, good food, very well organized, English, German and Dutch spoken, pioneers in mountain biking in Ecuador.

Bicycle shops Bike Stop, 6 de Diciembre N34-113 e Irlanda,T224 1192, www.bikestop.com.ec.
La Casa del Ciclista, Eloy Alfaro 1138 y República, T254 0339. Open daily. Sales, repairs and rentals (US$2 per hr, US$12 per day).
The Bike Shop, Río Coca y Los Shyris, CC Paseo del Río 13, T227 0330.

Horse riding

APROSAR, T269 9508 (evenings) or T09-903 0887. An association of 7 local horse-people, offers guided rides from just above the gate of the teleférico (see page 26), to a waterfall nearby or longer rides to Rucu Pichincha or beyond, US$10 per hr. Book ahead for large groups and long rides.
Green Horse Ranch, see page 55.
Juan Carlos Andrade, T246 4694, www.horsebackriding.com.ec. Rides from the teleférico to Rucu Pichincha returning via an hacienda, US$45 for 4 hrs, minimum 4 riders, reserve in advance.
Ride Andes, T09-973 8 221, www.rideandes. com. Private and set-date tours in the highlands including stays in haciendas, also in other South American countries.

Paragliding

Escuela Pichincha de Vuelo Libre, Carlos Endara Oe3-60 y Amazonas, T225 6592 (office hours), T09-993 1206, parapent@ uio.satnet.net. Offers complete courses for US$400 and tandem flights for US$60.

Swimming

There are a number of good, clean, heated public pools in the city. Swimming cap, towel and soap are compulsory for admission.
Miraflores, at the upper end of Av Universitaria, Tue-Sun 0900-1600. **Batán Alto**, Cochapata y Abascal, off Gaspar de Villaroel. **Colegio Benalcázar**, 6 de Diciembre y Portugal, also sauna. **La Cascada**, Flores N41-47 y Chile, T295 8200, also spa.

Tour operators

National park fees are rarely included in prices.
Advantage Travel, El Telégafo E10-63 y Juan de Alcántara, T246 2871, www.advantagecuador. com. Tours to Machalilla and Isla de la Plata. Also 4-5 day tours on a floating hotel on Río Napo.
Andando Tours – Angermeyer Cruises, Mariana de Jesús E7-113 y Pradera, T323 7186, www.andandotours.com. Operate several Galápagos vessels (*Mary Anne*, *Sagitta*) and tours in the highlands near Quito.

Andean Travel Company, Amazonas N24-03 y Wilson, p 3, T222 8385, www.andeantc.com. Dutch/Ecuadorean- owned operator, offers a wide range of tours including trekking, trips to **Cotococha Amazon Lodge** and cruises on the *Galapagos Voyager*, *Galapagos Odyssey* and *Galapagos Journey* vessels.

Andes Explorer, Reina Victoria 927 y Pinto, T290 1493, www.andes-explorer.com. Good-value budget mountain and jungle trips and sells Galápagos tours.

Campo Base, T259 9737, www.campobase-ecuador.com. Climbing, trekking and cycling tours, run by Manuel and Diego Jácome, very experienced climbing guides, they also have a mountain lodge 15 km south of Sangolquí, good for acclimatization at 3050 m.

Campus Trekking, Joaquina Vargas 99 y Calderón, Conocoto, Valle de los Chillos, T234 0601, www.campustrekking.com.ec. Good value trekking, climbing and cultural tours, 8- to 15-day biking trips, tailor-made itineraries, Galápagos. Also run **Hostería Pantaví** near Ibarra, 8 languages spoken.

Climbing Tours, Amazonas N21-221 y Roca, T254 4358, www.climbingtour.com. Climbing, trekking and other adventure sports, tours to regional attractions, also sell Galápagos and jungle tours.

Creter Tours, Pinto E5-29 y JL Mera, T254 5491, www.cretertours.com.ec. Operate the *Treasure of Galapagos* catamaran and sell many land tours.

Compañía de Guías, 9 de Octubre N21-179 y Roca, p2, T290 1551, www.companiadeguias. com. Climbing and trekking specialists, but sell other tours, English, German, French and Italian spoken.

Cotopaxi Cara Sur, at **Alta Montaña** , Washington E8-20 y 6 de Diciembre, T252 4422, T09-800 2681, www.cotopaxi carasur.com. Both experienced operators offering climbing and trekking tours, also own Albergue Cara Sur on Cotopaxi.

Dracaena, Pinto 446 y Amazonas, T254 6590, www.dracaenaecuador.com. Runs good budget jungle tours to Cuyabeno and climbing and trekking trips, popular.

EcoAndes, Baquedano E5-27 y JL Mera, T255 7650, www.ecoandestravel.com. Run by experienced guide Hugo Torres, for classic tours, adventure travel, Galápagos and Amazon. Also operate hotels in Quito.

Ecoventura, Almagro N31-80 y Whymper, T290 7396, www.ecoventura.com. Operate first-class Galápagos cruises and sell tours throughout Ecuador.

Ecuador Journeys, Cordero 1204 y JL Mera, p9, T254 9684, www.ecuadorianjourney.com, www.cheapgalapagoscruises.com. Adventure tours to off-the-beaten-path destinations, choice of day tours, treks to volcanos including Reventador, jungle trips.

Ecuador Treasure, Amazonas N24-157 y Calama, T223 6607, www.ecuadortreasure. com. Climbing, horse riding, cycling and cultural tours, sell Galápagos and jungle and run **Chuquirahua Lodge** in El Chaupi, near Reserva Los Ilinizas.

Ecuadorian Tours, Amazonas N21-33 y Washington, several other locations, T256 0488, www.ecuadoriantours.com. Airline tickets and tours in all regions.

Enchanted Expeditions, de las Alondras N45- 102 y de los Lirios, T334 0525, www.enchanted expeditions.com. Operate the *Cachalote* and *Beluga* Galápagos vessels, sell jungle trips to Cuyabeno and highland tours. Very experienced.

Equateur Voyages Passion, in L'Auberge Inn, Gran Colombia N15-200 y Yaguachi, T254 3803, www.equateur-voyages.com. Full range of adventure tours, run a 4- to 5-day jungle tour on the Shiripuno River, sell Galápagos cruises.

Exclusive Hotels & Haciendas of Ecuador, 12 de Octubre y Orellana E11-14 , p2, 254 4719, www.ehhec.com. A reservation centre for a range of high-end hotels, haciendas, lodges and spas, also offer private transport in 4WD vehicles with English-speaking chauffeur/guide from US$170 per day.

Galacruises Expeditions, 9 de Octubre N22-118 y Veintimilla, T252 3324, www.galacruises.com. Offer Galápagos cruises on the *Sea Man II* catamaran and other vessels.

Galapagos Odyssey, Amazonas N24-03 y Wilson, 2p of 2, T286 0355, www.galapagos odyssey.com. Arranges cruises around the Galápagos islands as well as birdwatching and trekking.

Galasam, Cordero N24-214 y Amazonas, T290 3909, www.galasam.com. Has a fleet of boats in different categories for Galápagos cruises. City tours, full range of highland tours and jungle trips to **Siona Lodge** in Cuayabeno.

Galextur, Portugal E10-271 y 6 de Diciembre, T226 9626, www.galextur.com. Run 4- to 8-day land-based Galápagos tours with daily sailings to different islands and **Hotel Silberstein** in Puerto Ayora. Good service.

Geo Reisen, El Telégrafo E9-39 y Juan de Alcántara, T244 6224. Specializing in cultural, adventure and nature tours adapted for individuals, groups or families.

Gulliver, JL Mera N24-156 y José Calama, T252 9297, www.gulliver.com.ec. Wide range of options from guided vehicle tours to extreme outdoor pursuits. Operate **Hostería Papagayo** south of Quito and **Cocoa Inn** near Puerto Quito. Also sell Galápagos and jungle tours and airline tickets.

Happy Gringo, Foch E6-12 y Reina Victoria, T222 0031, www.happygringo.com. Open daily. Operate tours to Otavalo and in Quito and surroundings. Sell Galápagos, jungle and other tours, good service.

Humboldt Expeditions, see Andando Tours above for contact information. Cultural, nature and adventure tours in Quito and the highlands.

Kempery Tours, Ramírez Dávalos 117 y Amazonas, Ed Turismundial, p 2, T250 5599, www.kempery.com. Good-value tours, 4- to 14-day jungle trips to **Bataburo Lodge** in Huaorani territory, operate the *Angelique* and *Archipel II* vessels in Galápagos, multilingual service.

Klein Tours, Eloy Alfaro N34-151 y Catalina Aldaz, also Shyris N34-280 y Holanda, T226 7000, www.kleintours.com. Operate the *Galapagos Legend* and *Coral I* and *II* cruise ships also **Chiva Don Otto** Quito city tour (page 38) and **Chaski Antawa** train (page 77). Tailor-made itineraries, English, French and German spoken.

Latin Trails, Rumiñahui 221 y 1ra Transversal, San Rafael, T286 7832, www.latintrails.com, www.galapagos catamarans.com. Run the *Galapagos Journey I* and *II* catamarans and offer a variety of land trips in several countries.

Latitud 0°, Mallorca N24-500 y Coruña, La Floresta, T254 7921, www.latitud0.com. Climbing specialists, French spoken.

Mallku Expeditions, 10 de Agosto N26-117 y Aguirre, T255 0090, www.mallkuexpeditions.com. Operate the *Daphne* Galápagos yacht, a hostel in Puerto Ayora and sell tours in Ecuador and Peru.

Metropolitan Touring, Av Las Palmeras N45-74 y Las Orquídeas, Amazonas N20-39 y 18 de Septiembre and at shopping centres, T298 8200, www.metropolitan-touring.com. A large organization that operates tours throughout Ecuador and Peru, Chile and Argentina. Operate several luxury Galápagos vessels, **Finch Bay Hotel** in Puerto Ayora and the *Chiva Express* private rail journey along the Devil's Nose route. Also adventure, cultural and gastronomy tours.

PalmarVoyages, Alemania N31-77 y Mariana de Jesús, T256 9809, www.palmar voyages.com. Experienced tour operator, tailor-made itineraries in Ecuador and other Latin American countries, adventure tours, jungle expeditions, Galápagos trips, flight tickets, attentive service, good rates.

Positiv Turismo, Jorge Juan N33-38 y Atahualpa, T600 9401, www.positivturismo. com. Swiss/Austrian-run company. Galápagos, cultural trips, trekking and special interest tours.

Quasar Náutica, José Jussieu N41-28 y Alonso de Torres, T244 6996, T1-800 247

2925 (USA), www.quasarnautica.com. Highly recommended 7- to 10-day naturalist and diving Galápagos cruises on 8- to 16-berth luxury yachts.

Rolf Wittmer Turismo/Tip Top Travel, Foch E7- 81 y Almagro, T252 6938, www.rwittmer.com. Run 1st-class yachts: *Tip Top II*, *III* and *IV*. Also tailor-made tours throughout Ecuador.

Safari, Colón y Reina Victoria N25-33, p 11, of 1101, T255 2505, www.safari.com.ec. Excellent adventure travel, specialized out-of-the-ordinary itineraries, climbing, cycling, rafting, trekking and cultural tours. Also book Galápagos tours, sell jungle trips and run a glacier school. A good source of travel information. Recommended. Daily 0930-1830.

Sangay Touring, Cordero E4-358, T255 0176, www.sangay.com. Operate a variety of custom-designed tours, particularly in Oriente, and sell Galápagos trips, efficient service.

Sierra Nevada, Pinto E4-150 y Cordero, T252 8264, www.sierranevada.ec. Specialized multiple-day adventure expeditions: climbing, trekking, rafting and jungle, experienced multilingual guides, good service.

Surtrek, Amazonas N23-87 y Wilson, T250 0530, www.surtrek.com. Custom designed trips with personalized itineraries for individuals and small groups, cultural and adventure trips throughout Ecuador, Galápagos tours, also sell domestic flights and run **Las Cascadas Lodge**.

Terrasenses, C E2C y N90A No 709, T344 1682 or T09-821 5621, www.terrasenses.com. Cultural, adventure and nature tours for groups of 2 to 10, honeymoon tours and destination weddings.

Tierra de Fuego, Amazonas N23-23 y Veintimilla, T250 1418, www.ecuadortierra defuego.com. Provide transport and tours throughout the country, domestic flight tickets and Galápagos bookings (www.galapagosprograms.com).

Tours Unlimited, Julio Castro E6-16 y Valparaíso, T252 5834, www.tours-unlimited. com. Custom-made itineraries in all regions, city and regional tours including the Tulipe-Pachijal private cloudforest reserve, www.tulipecloudforest.org, Galápagos bookings, operate **The Guest House** in Quito.

Tropic Journeys in Nature, La Niña E7-46 y Almagro, T222 5907, www.tropiceco.com. Environmental and cultural tours to the **Huaorani Ecolodge**, the highlands, coast and Galápagos, including walking tours on Isabela. Founder Andy Drumm works closely with conservation and indigenous groups. General Manager is Jascivan Carvalho. A percentage of all profits supports **Conservation in Action**. Winner of several awards for responsible tourism.

Zenith Travel, JL Mera N24-234 y Cordero, T252 9993, www.zenithecuador.com. Economical Galápagos cruises as well as various land tours in Ecuador and Peru. All-gay Galápagos cruises available. Multilingual service, knowledgeable helpful staff, good value.

Whitewater rafting

Ríos Ecuador/Yacu Amu, Foch 746 y JL Mera, T290 4054, www.riosecuador.com. Australian-owned (Steve Nomchong), very professional, rafting and kayaking trips of 1-6 days, also kayak courses, good equipment. For Grade IV and V runs, contact freelance guide **Dan Dixon** here. Highly recommended.

Sierra Nevada (see Tour operators, above), excellent trips from 1-3 days, chief guide Edison Ramírez (fluent English/French) is certified by French Association.

All charge about US$50-80 per day.

Mitad del Mundo *p27*

Calimatours, Manzana de los Correos, Of 11, Mitad del Mundo, T239 4796, www.calima ecuador.com. Tours to all the sites in the vicinity. Offers beautiful certificates to record your visit. Recommended.

Quito *p17, maps p16, p21 and p24*
Air
Mariscal Sucre Airport, T294 4900,
www.quiport.com. Details of internal air
service are given in the respective
destinations; see also www.ecuador
schedules.com. There is a hotel booking
service at international arrivals. **Moneyzone**
cambio in international departures, open
0430-2100, poor rates for 12 currencies. There
are duty-free shops in the international
departures lounge. A new airport is
scheduled to open in 2011-2012. The safest
and easiest way to travel between airport and
town is by **taxi**. You can catch one from the
rank outside arrivals. Buy a ticket first at the
booth inside internatioanl arrivals: fixed fare
from the airport to La Mariscal US$6; to the
colonial city US$8; to Quitumbe terminal
US$15; to Carcelén terminal US$6.
Alternatively, the **Trans-Rabbit** or **Achupallas**
van services are good value for groups of 4 or
more. Individuals who buy a ticket for a van
must either pay more or wait until they get
enough passengers. **Public buses** are not
recommended unless you have virtually no
luggage or are desperately low on funds.
Buses and trolley alike are too crowded to
enter with even a small backpack so the risk
of theft is very high. The bus stop is 1 block
west of terminal, in front of Centro Comercial
Aeropuerto. For modern Quito take a
southbound bus marked 'Carcelén-Congreso',
fare US$0.25. For colonial Quito take a green
alimentador (feeder bus line) from the same
stop to the northern terminus of the trolley
line, combined fare US$0.25. There is no bus
or trolley service late at night when most
flights from North America arrive.

Bus
Local Quito has 3 parallel mass transit lines
running from north to south on exclusive
lanes, covering almost the length of the city.

Feeder bus lines (*alimentadores*) go from the
terminals to outer suburbs. Within the city the
fare is US$0.25; the combined fare to some
suburbs is US$0.40. **Trole** (T266 5016, Mon-Fri
0500-2345, weekends and holidays
0600-2145, plus hourly overnight service with
limited stops) is a system of trolley buses
which runs along Av 10 de Agosto in the
north of the city, C Guayaquil (southbound)
and C Flores (northbound) in colonial Quito,
and mainly along Av Maldonado and Av
Teniente Ortiz in the south. The northern
terminus is north of 'La Y', the junction of 10
de Agosto, Av América and Av de la Prensa;
south of the colonial city are important
transfer stations at El Recreo, known as
Terminal Sur, and Morán Valverde; the
southern terminus is at the Quitumbe bus
station. Trolleys do not necessarily run the full
length of the line, the destination is marked in
front of the vehicle. Trolleys have a special
entrance for wheelchairs. **Ecovía** (T243 0726,
Mon-Sat 0500-2200, Sun and holidays
0600-2200), articulated buses, runs along Av
6 de Diciembre from Estación Río Coca, at C
Río Coca east of 6 de Diciembre, in the north,
to La Marín transfer station, east of colonial
Quito. The route will be extended to the
south along Av Napo. **Metrobus** (T346 5149,
Mon-Fri 0530-2230, weekends and holidays
0600-2100) also runs articulated buses along
Av de la Prensa and Av América from
Terminal La Ofelia in the north to La Marín in
the south. There are plans to extend the
Ecovía and Metrobus lines. There are also 2
types of **city buses**: *Selectivos* are red, take
mostly sitting passengers and a limited
number standing and *Bus Tipo* are royal blue,
take sitting and standing passengers, both
cost US$0.25. Many bus lines go through La
Marín and El Playón Ecovía/Metrobus
stations. Extra caution is advised here: it is a
rough area, pickpockets abound and it is best
avoided at night.
  Short distance Outer suburbs are served
by green *Interparroquial* buses. Those

running east to the valleys of Cumbayá, Tumbaco and beyond leave from the Estación Río Coca (see Ecovía above). Buses southeast to Valle de los Chillos leave from El Playón Ecovía/Metrobus station and from Isabel la Católica y Mena Caamaño, behind Universidad Católica. Buses going north (ie Calderón, Mitad del Mundo) leave from La Ofelia Metrobus station. Regional destinations to the north (ie Cayambe) and northwest (ie Mindo) leave from a regional station adjacent to La Ofelia Metrobus station. Buses south to Machachi from La Villaflora and Quitumbe. Buses to Baeza and El Chaco leave from Don Bosco E1-136 y Av Pichincha in La Marín.

Long distance 2 modern terminals opened in 2009. **Terminal Quitumbe** in the southwest of the city, T398 8200, for destinations south, the coast via Santo Domingo, Oriente and Tulcán (in the north). It is served by the Trole (line 4: El Ejido-Quitumbe, best taken at El Ejido) and the Metrobus is being extended towards it, however it is advisable to take a taxi, about US$6, 30-45 mins to the colonial city, US$8-10, 45 mins-1 hr to La Mariscal. Arrivals, tourist information, phone/internet office, bank, ATMs and Trole entrance are on the ground floor. Ticket counters (destinations grouped and colour coded by region), departures and ATMs are at the upper level. Left luggage (US$0.90 per day) and food stalls are at the adjoining shopping area. The terminal is large, allow extra time to reach your bus. Terminal use fee US$0.20. Watch your belongings at all times. On holiday weekends it is advisable to reserve the day before. The smaller **Terminal Carcelén**, Av Eloy Alfaro, where it meets the Panamericana Norte, T3961600, serves destinations to the north (including Otavalo) and the coast via the Calacalí– La Independencia road. It is served by feeder bus lines from the northern terminals of the Trole, Ecovía and Metrobus, a taxi costs

about US$3, 30-45 mins to La Mariscal, US$7, 45 mins-1hr to colonial Quito. Ticket counters are organized by destination. See under destinations for fares and schedules; see also www.ecuadorschedules.com. A convenient way to travel between Quitumbe and Carcelén is to take a bus bound for Tulcán, **Trans Vencedores** or **Unión del Carchi** (Booth 12), every 30 mins during the day, hourly at night, US$1, 1 hr; from Carcelén to Quitumbe, wait for a through bus arriving from the north; taxi between terminals, US$15. There are plans for direct city buses between terminals, these were not running at the time of writing.

Several companies run better quality coaches on the longer routes, those with terminals in modern Quito are: **Flota Imbabura**, Larrea 1211 y Portoviejo, T223 6940, for **Cuenca** and **Guayaquil**; **Transportes Ecuador**, JL Mera N21-44 y Washington, T250 3842, to **Guayaquil**; **Transportes Esmeraldas**, Santa María 870 y Amazonas, T250 9517, for **Esmeraldas**, **Atacames**, **Coca**, **Lago Agrio**, **Manta** and **Huaquillas**. Reina del Camino, Larrea y 18 de Septiembre, T321 6633, for **Bahía**, **Puerto López** and **Manta**; Carlos Aray Larrea y Portoviejo, T256 4406, for **Manta** and **Puerto López**; Transportes Occidentales, 18 de Septiembre y Versalles, T250 2733, for **Esmeraldas**, Atacames, **Salinas** and **Lago Agrio**; TAC, Almagro y Pinta, for **Zaruma** and **Machala**; COACTUR, same address as TAC, for **Portoviejo**; Transportes Baños, for **Baños** and Oriente destinations, has a ticket counter at Santa María y JL Mera, but buses leave from Quitumbe. Panamericana Internacional, Colón E7-31 y Reina Victoria, T255 7133, ext 126 for national routes, ext 125 for international, for **Huaquillas**, **Machala**, **Cuenca**, **Loja**, **Guayaquil**, **Manta** and **Esmeraldas**. They also run an international service: 4 weekly to **Bogotá**, changing buses in Tulcán and Ipiales, US$85, 28 hrs; **Caracas**, 1 weekly, US$130, 3 days; to **Lima**, daily, changing buses in Aguas Verdes and Túmbes, US$85, 38 hrs. **Ormeño Internacional**, from Perú, Shyris N34-432 y Portugal, T246 0027, Tue and Thu 0200 to **Lima** US$80, **La Paz**, US$170, 2½ days, **Santiago** US$210, 4 days, **Buenos Aires** US$280, 6 days, To **Cali**, 2 weekly, US$50 and **Bogotá** US$70. To **Caracas**, 1 weekly, US$100. **Rutas de América**, Selva Alegre Oe1-72 y 10 de Agosto, T250 3611, www.rutasenbus. com, to **Lima**, 1 weekly, US$65; to **Caracas**, 2 weekly, US$135, 2½ days, does not go into Colombian cities, but will let passengers off by the roadside (eg Popayán, Palmira for Cali or Ibagué for Bogotá, all US$55). The route to **Peru** via Loja and Macará takes much longer than the Huaquillas route, but is more relaxed. Don't buy Peruvian (or any other country's) bus tickets here, they're much cheaper outside Ecuador.

Shared taxis and vans offer door-to-door service and avoid the hassle of reaching Quito bus terminals. Reserve at least 2 days ahead. **Taxis Lagos** shared taxis to **Otavalo** and **Ibarra**, www.taxislagos.com, see page 66. **Lucy Express**, T09-786 4264, www.lucyexpress.com, daily vans to **Guayaquil**, US$21.50, excellent comfortable service with a/c. **Traex Turey**, T03-242 6828 (Ambato) or T09-924 2795, 8 daily departures to **Ambato** (US$12), they will also drop passengers off in **Latacunga** (US$10), or continue to **Baños** (US$20 extra per vehicle). **Montecarlo Trans Vip**, T03-294 3054 (Riobamba) or T08-411 4114, 3 daily to **Riobamba**, US$15. **Sudamericana Taxis**, to **Santo Domingo**.

Taxi

Taxis are a safe, cheap (from US$1) and efficient way to get around the city. For airport and bus terminal taxis, see above. All taxis must have working meters by law, but make sure the meter is running (if it isn't, fix the fare before). Expect to pay US$1-2 more at night when meter may not be used. All legally registered taxis have the number of their co-operative and the individual operator's number prominently painted on the side of the vehicle and on a sticker on the windshield. They are safer and cheaper than unauthorized taxis. Note the registration and the licence plate numbers if you feel you have been seriously overcharged or mistreated. You may then complain to the transit police or tourist office. Be reasonable and remember that the majority of taxi drivers are honest and helpful. At night it is safer to use a radio taxi, there are several companies including: **Taxi Amigo**, T222 2222; **City Taxi**, T263 3333; and **Central de Radio Taxis**, T250 0600. Make sure they give you the taxi number so that you get the correct vehicle, some radio taxis are unmarked. To hire a taxi by the hour costs from US$7 in the city, from US$9 outside town. For trips outside Quito, agree the fare beforehand: US$70-85 a day. Outside luxury hotels cooperative taxi drivers have a list of agreed excursion prices and most drivers are knowledgeable. For taxi tours with a guide, try **Hugo Herrera**, T226 7891. He speaks English and is recommended.

Train

Regular passenger service has been discontinued throughout the country. A tourist train runs from **Quito** to **Latacunga**, Wed, Fri-Sun and holidays at 0730, returns 1400. US$10 return, children under 12 and seniors US$5, Purchase tickets in advance from **Empresa de Ferrocarriles Ecuatorianos**, Bolívar Oe5-43 y García Moreno, colonial Quito, T258 2930 or T1-800-873637, www.efe.gov.ec, Mon-Fri 0830-1630, you need each passenger's passport number and age to purchase tickets. You can alight at any of the stops and will be picked up on the return trip. The tour starts at the lovely refurbished

Language schools in Quito

Quito is one of the most important centres for Spanish language study in Latin America with over 80 schools operating. There is a great variety to choose from. Identify your budget and goals for the course: rigorous grammatical and technical training, fluent conversation skills, getting to know Ecuadoreans or just enough basic Spanish to get you through your trip.

Visit a few places to get a feel for what they charge and offer. Prices vary greatly, from US$4 to US$12 per hour, but you do not always get what you pay for. There is also tremendous variation in teacher qualifications, infrastructure and resource materials. Schools usually offer courses of four or seven hours tuition per day. Many correspondents suggest that four is enough. Some schools offer packages which combine teaching in the morning and touring in the afternoon, others combine teaching with travel to various attractions throughout the country. A great deal of emphasis has traditionally been placed on one-to-one teaching, but

remember that a well-structured small classroom setting can also be very good.

The quality of homestays likewise varies, the cost including meals runs from US$12 to US$25 per day. Try to book just one week at first to see how a place suits you. For language courses as well as homestays, deal directly with the people who will provide services to you, avoid intermediaries and always get a detailed receipt.

If you are short on time then it can be a good idea to make your arrangements from home, either directly with one of the schools or through an agency, who can offer you a wide variety of options. If you have more time and less money, then it may be more economical to organize your own studies after you arrive. South American Explorers provides a list (free to members) of recommended schools and these may give club members discounts.

We list schools for which we have received positive recommendations each year. This does not imply that schools not mentioned are not recommended.

Estación Chimbacalle (Maldonado y Sincholagua, 2 km south of the colonial city, T265 6142), with a visit to a railway museum. There is a breakfast stop at either **Tambillo** or **Machachi**, next stop is **El Boliche**, with views of Cotopaxi and Los Ilinizas. If you wish to spend a few hours until the train returns at about 1500, here is **Área Nacional de Recreación El Boliche** entrance fee US$10, a protected area abutting on Parque Nacional Cotopaxi. The train continues to **Latacunga**, where you have a couple of hours until the return trip leaves at 1400. You cannot purchase tickets to board at Latacunga. **Metropolitan Touring** and **Klein Tours**, see above, offer tours involving train travel.

Mitad del Mundo and around *p27*
Bus From Quito take a 'Mitad del Mundo' feeder bus from La Ofelia station on the Metrobus (transfer ticket US$0.15). Some buses continue to the turn-off for Pululahua or Calacalí beyond. An excursion by **taxi** to Mitad del Mundo (with 1-hr wait) is US$25, or US$30 to include Pululahua. Just a ride from La Mariscal costs about US$15.

ℹ Directory

Quito *p17, maps p16, p21 and p24*
Airline offices National: Aerogal/VIP, Amazonas 607 y Carrión, República de El Salvador y Suiza and booths at Quicentro Shopping and CCI, T294 2800 and

1-800-237642, www.aerogal. com.ec. **Icaro**, JL Mera N26-221 y Orellana, Los Shyris N34-108 y Holanda, T299 7400, T1-800-883567. **TAME**, Amazonas N24-260 y Colón and 12 de Octubre N24-383 y Baquerizo Moreno, T1-800-500800. **International: Air France/ KLM**, 12 de Octubre N26-27 y Lincoln, T298 6820. **American**, Amazonas 4545 y Pereira and booth at Mall El Jardín, T299 5000. **Avianca**, Bello Horizonte E11-44 y Coruña, T1-800- 003434. **Continental**, 12 de Octubre 1942 y Cordero, World Trade Center, Mezzanine and Naciones Unidas E10-44 y 6 de Diciembre, T225 0905, 1-800-222333. **Copa**, República de El Salvador N31-201 y Moscú, T227 3082. **Delta**, Los Shyris y Suecia, edif Renazzo Plaza PB, T333 1691 T1-800-101080. **Iberia**, Eloy Alfaro 939 y Amazonas, edif Finandes, p 5, T256 6009. **LAN**, Orellana E11-28 y Coruña and Quicentro Shopping, T299 2300, 1-800-101075. **Santa Bárbara**, República de El Salvador 354 y Moscú, T02-227 9650. **TACA**, República de El Salvador N36-139 y Suecia, T292 3170, T1-800-008222.

Banks The highest concentration of banks and ATMs is in modern Quito. Many are along Av Amazonas, both in La Mariscal and La Carolina, and along Naciones Unidas between Amazonas and Los Shyris. In colonial Quito there are banks near the main plazas. To change TCs, casas de cambio and **Banco del Pacífico**, Naciones Unidas E7-95 y Shyris and Amazonas y Veintimilla. **Casas de cambio**: All open Mon-Fri 0900-1730, Sat 0900-1245. **Euromoney**, Amazonas N21-229 y Roca, T252 6907. Change 10 currencies, 2% commission for Amex US$ TCs **Mega Cambios**, Amazonas N24-01 y Wilson, T255 5849. 3% commission for US$ TCs, change cash euros, sterling, Canadian dollars. **Vazcorp**, Amazonas N21-169 y Roca, T252 9212. Change 11 currencies, 1.8% comission for US$ TCs, good rates, recommended. **Car hire** All the main car rental companies are at the airport. City offices of local companies: **Expo**, Av América N21-66 y Bolívia, T222

8688, T1-800-736822. **Rent 4WD**, 12 de Octubre E11-14 y Orellana, p 2, T254 4719, www.rent- 4wd.com. 4WD vehicles with driver, from US$170 per day all inclusive. **Simon Car Rental**, Los Shyris 2930 e Isla Floreana, T243 1019, good rates and service. **Achupallas Tours**, T330 1493, and **Trans-Rabbit**, T330 1496, both at the international arrivals section of the Airport, rent vans for 8-14 passengers, with driver, for trips in Quito and out of town. **Cultural centres Alliance Française**, Eloy Alfaro N32-468, T245 2017, www.afquito.org.ec. French courses, films and cultural events. **Casa Humboldt**, Vancouver E5-54 y Polonia, T02-254 8480, www.asociacion-humboldt.org. Goethe Institute, films, theatre, exhibitions. **Centro Cultural Con Manos de Ebano**, 6 de Diciembre N23-43 y Baquedano, T222 8969, www.azucarafroe.com. Cultural events run by Afro- Ecuadorean community, also restaurant. **Damas Norteamericanas y Británicas**, 12 de Octubre N26-138 y Orellana, T222 8190. The Library, Wed-Sat 1000-1200 plus Fri 1500-1700, is an excellent resource, non- members can join, a charitable foundation, deposite required. **Embassies and consulates Austria**, Gaspar de Villaroel E9-53 y Los Shyris, p 3, T244 3272, przibra@interactive. net.ec, 1000-1200. **Belgium** (Cooperation office), República de El Salvador 1082 y Naciones Unidas, p 10, T227 6145, www.diplomatie.be/ quitoes. Consular affairs handled in Lima. **Canada**, Amazonas N37-29 y Unión Nacional de Periodistas, p 3, T245 5499, www.quito.gc.ca, 0900-1200. **Colombia** (consulate), Atahualpa 955 y República, edif Digicom p 3, T245 8012, consuladoenquito@andinanet.net. 0900-1300 1400-1600. **Finland**, Whimper N30-91 y Coruña, T290 1501. **France**, Plaza 107 y Patria, T294 3800, www.amba france-ec.org. Mon-Thu 0900-1300. 1430-1730, Fri 0830-1330. **Germany**, Naciones Unidas E10-44 y República de El Salvador, edif City Plaza, T297 0820, www.quito.diplo.de. 0830-1130. **Ireland**, Yanacocha y Juan Prócel, El Condado, T600 1166, dominiquekennedy@gmail.com, 0900-1200. **Israel**, Coruña E25-58 y San Ignacio,T397 1500, http://quito.mfa.gov.il, 0900-1300. **Italy**, La Isla 111 y H Albornoz, T256 1077, www.ambitalquito.org. 0830-1230. **Japan**, Amazonas N39-123 y Arízaga, p11, T227 8700, 0930-1200, 1400-1700. **Netherlands**, 12 de Octubre 1942 y Cordero, World Trade Center, p 1, T222 9229, http://ecuador.nlambassade.org, 0830-1300, 1400-1730. **Norway**, República de El Salvador 1082 y Naciones Unidas, Ed Mansión Blanca, Torre París, p4, T2461523, 0900-1200. **Peru**, República de El Salvador N34-361 e Irlanda, T246 8410, www.embajadadelperu.org.ec, 0900-1300, 1500-1800. **Spain**, La Pinta 455 y Amazonas, T256 4373. 0900-1200. **Sweden**, Almagro N32-27 y Whymper, edif TorresWhymper p11, T223 3793, vconsuec@uio.satnet.net, Mon-Thu 0930-1230. **Switzerland**, Juan Pablo Sanz 3617 y Amazonas, edif Xerox p 2, T243 4949, www.eda.admin.ch/quito. 0900-1200. **United Kingdom**, Naciones Unidas y República de El Salvador, edif Citiplaza, p 14, T297 0800. Mon-Thu 0800-1230, 1330-1600, Fri 0830-1230. **USA**, Av Avigiras E12-170 y Eloy Alfaro, T398 5000, http://ecuador. usembassy.gov. 0800-1230, 1330-1700. **Internet** Quito has very many cybercafés, particularly in La Mariscal. Rates start at about US$0.60 per hr, but US$1 is more typical. **Language schools** The following schools have received favourable reports. **In modern Quito: Academia de Español Quito**, Marchena Oe1-30 y 10 de Agosto, T255 3647, www.academiaquito.edu.ec. **Amazonas**, Washington 718 y Amazonas, edif Rocafuerte, p3, T250 4654, www.eduamazonas.com. **Andean Global Studies**, El Mercurio E10-23 y la Razón, T02-225 4928 www.andeanglobal studies.org. Customized travel-study programs. **Atahualpa**, Godín N20-29 y Condaminehabla@atahualpa.com. **Beraca**, Amazonas N24-66 y Pinto, p 2, T290 6642, www.beraca.net. **Bipo & Toni's**, Carrión E8-183 y Plaza, T254 7090, www.bipo.net. **Cristóbal Colón**, Colón Oe2-56 y Versalles, T250 6508, www.colonspanishschool.com. Also offer courses in Baños, Otavalo, Cuenca and Manta, and run **Tutamanda Hostel** (www.tutamanda hostel.com). **EIL Ecuador**, Hernando de la Cruz N31-37 y Mariana de Jesúseil@eilecuador.org. **Equinox**, Pinzón N25-106 y Colón, T222 6544, www.ecuador spanish.com. Small school. **Instituto Superior de Español**, Darquea Terán 1650 y 10 de Agosto, T222 3242, www.instituto-superior. net. Also have schools in Otavalo (Sucre 11-10 y Morales, p 2, T06-292 2414) and Galápagos (advanced booking required). **La Lengua**, Colón 1001 y JL Mera, p 8, T250 1271, www.la- lengua.com. Also have a school at Puerto López (book in advance) and offer a 4 week study and travel programme. Recommended. **Mitad del Mundo**, Barrio Ponceano Calle C N71-193 y Calle B, in northern Quito, T254 6827, www.mitad mundo.com.ec. Offer special courses for business, health and other professionals. Repeatedly recommended. **Quito S.I. Spanish Institute**, 9 de Octubre N27-09 y Orellana, T255 0377, www.quitospanish.com. Spanish courses and examination centre for DELE Spanish proficiency diplomas. **Simón Bolívar**, Foch E9-20 y 6 de Diciembreinfo@simon- bolivar.com. **Sintaxis**, 10 de Agosto N20-53 y Bolivia, edif Andrade, p 5, T252 0006, www.sintaxis.net. Consistently recommended. **South American**, Amazonas N26-59 y Santa María, T254 2715, www.southamerican. edu.ec. Also have a school in Guayaquil. **Universidad Católica**, 12 de Octubre y Roca, Sección de Español, T299 1700 ext 1388, mejaramillo@puce.edu.ec. **Vida Verde**, Plaza N23-100 y Wilson, T02-222 6635, www.vidaverde.com. Part of profits go to support social and environmental projects.

Medical services Most embassies have the telephone numbers of doctors and dentists who speak non-Spanish languages.
Hospitals: Hospital Voz Andes Villalengua Oe 2-37 y Av 10 de Agosto, T226 2142 (Trole, la Y stop). Emergency room, quick and efficient, fee based on ability to pay, run by Christian HCJB organization, has outpatient dept, T243 9343. **Hospital Metropolitano**, Mariana de Jesús y Occidental, T226 1520, ambulance T226 5020. Very professional and recommended, but expensive. **Clínica Pichincha**, Veintimilla E3-30 y Páez, T256 2296, ambulance T250 1565. Another very good, expensive hospital. **Clínica Pasteur**, Eloy Alfaro 552 y 9 de Octubre, T223 4004. Also good and cheaper than the above. **Novaclínica Santa Cecilia**, Veintimilla 1394 y 10 de Agosto, T254 5390, emergency T254 5000. Reasonable prices, good. **Med Center Travel Clinic** (Dr John Rosenberg), Foch 476 y Almagro, T252 1104, 09-973 9734. General and travel medicine with a full range of vaccines, speaks English and German, very helpful GP. **Fybeca** is a reliable chain of 33 pharmacies throughout the city. Their 24-hr branches are at Amazonas y Tomás de Berlanga near the Plaza de Toros, and at C C El Recreo in the south. **Post offices** All branches open Mon-Fri 0800-1800, Sat 0800-1200. In principle all branches provide all services, but your best chances are at Colón y Almagro in the Mariscal district, and at the main sorting centre on Japón near Naciones Unidas, behind the CCI shopping centre. The branch on Eloy Alfaro 354 y 9 de Octubre frequently loses mail; best avoided. There is also a branch in the colonial city, on Espejo entre Guayaquil y Venezuela. The branch at Ulloa and Ramírez Dávalos, behind Mercado Santa Clara is the centre for parcel post, and you may be directed there to send large packages. Poste restante at the post offices at Espejo and at Eloy Alfaro (less efficient). All poste restante letters are sent to Espejo unless marked 'Correo Central, Eloy Alfaro', but you are advised to check both postes restantes, whichever address you use. **South American Explorers** hold mail for members. **Telephones** There are cabins (*cabinas*) all over the city for national and international calls. The latter will be cheaper from internet cafés. There are also debit cardcell phones throughout the city. **Useful addresses Emergencies:** T911 for all types of emergency in Quito. **Immigration Offices:** see Planning your trip. **Police:** T101. **Servicio de Seguridad Turística, Policía de Turismo**, Reina Victoria y Roca, T254 3983. Report robberies here. Also at **Fiscalía de Turismo, Ministerio de Turismo**, Eloy Alfaro N32-300 y Tobar, T250 7559 (ext 1018), Public Prosecutors Office, Mon-Fri 0800-1200, 1400-1800.

Around Quito

Papallacta → *Phone code: 06. Regional population: 1150. Altitude: 3200 m.*

At the **Termas de Papallacta** ① *64 km east from Quito, 2 km from the town of Papallacta, 0600-2100, T02-256 8989 (Quito), www.papallacta.com.ec*, the best developed hot springs in the country, are ten thermal pools, three large enough for swimming, and four cold plunge pools. There are two public complexes of springs: the **regular pools** ① *US$7*, and the **spa centre** ① *US$17 (massages and other special treatments extra)*. There are additional pools at the Termas hotel and cabins (see Sleeping, page 53) for the exclusive use of their guests. The complex is tastefully done and recommended. The view, on a clear day, of Antisana while enjoying the thermal waters is superb. There are several self-guided routes in the **Rancho del Cañón** ① *US$2 for use of a short trail, to go on longer walks you are required to take a guide for US$6-15 per person*, a private reserve behind the pools. To the north of this private reserve is **Reserva Cayambe Coca** ① *T/F02-211 0370, entry US$10*. A scenic road starts by the Termas information centre, crosses both reserves and leads in 45 km to Oyacachi. A permit from Cayambe Coca headquartes (request by fax) is required to travel this road even on foot. It is a lovely two-day walk, there is a ranger's station and camping area 1½ hours from Papallacta. Reserva Cayambe Coca is also accesed from La Virgen, the pass on the road to Quito. **Fundación Ecológica Rumicocha** ① *T02-321 4833, www.rumicocha.org.ec*, offers guiding service. In addition to the Termas there are municipal pools in the village of Papallacta and several more economical places to stay (some with pools) on the road to the Termas and in the village.

Refugio de Vida Silvestre Pasochoa
① *US$10, very busy at weekends, 45 mins southeast of Quito by car.*
This natural park set in humid Andean forest is run by the **Fundación Natura** ① *Elia Liut N45-10 y El Telégrafo, T227 2863 ext 328, www.fnatura.org*. Situated between 2700 m and 4200 m, the reserve has more than 120 species of birds (unfortunately some of the fauna has been frightened away by the noise of the visitors) and 50 species of trees. There are walks of 30 minutes to eight hours. There is a refuge (US$6-10 per person per night, with hot shower and cooking facilities) but take a sleeping bag; camping is US$4 per person. Meals must be requested in advance, or take food and water as there are no shops.

To the western slopes of Pichincha → *Altitude: 1200-2800 m.*
Despite their proximity to the capital (two hours from Quito), the western slopes of **Pichincha** and its surroundings are surprisingly wild, with fine opportunities for walking and birdwatching. This scenic area has lovely cloudforests and many nature reserves. The main tourist town in this area is Mindo. To the west of Mindo is a warm subtropical area of clear rivers and waterfalls, where a growing number of tourist developments are springing up.

Paseo del Quinde Two roads go from Quito northwest over the western Cordillera before dropping into the western lowlands. The old, rough route via Rundupamba, Nono (the only town of any size along this route) and Tandayapa, is dubbed the Paseo del Quinde or **Ecoruta** (Route of the Hummingbird), see www.ecorutadelquinde.org. It begins towards the northern end of Avenida Occidental, Quito's western ring road, at the intersection with Calle Machala. With increased awareness of the need to conserve the cloud forests of the northwest slopes of Pichincha and of their potential for tourism, the number of reserves here is steadily growing. Keen birdwatchers are no longer the only visitors, and the region has much to offer all nature lovers. Infrastructure at reserves varies considerably. Some have comfortable upmarket lodges offering accommodation, meals, guides and transport. Others may require taking your own camping gear, food, and obtaining a permit. There are too many reserves and lodges to mention here; see *Footprint Ecuador* for more details.

At Km 62 on the old road is **Bellavista Cloud Forest Reserve**, a 700-ha private reserve with excellent birdwatching and botany in the cloudforest. There are 20 km of trails ranging from wheelchair access to the slippery/suicidal. See **Hostería Bellavista** below.

The paved route From the Mitad del Mundo monument the road goes past **Calacalí**, whose plaza has an older monument to the Mitad del Mundo. Beyond Calacalí is a toll (US$0.80 for cars) where a road turns south to Nono and north to Yunguilla. Another road at Km 52 goes to Tandayapa and Bellavista. The main paved road, with heavy traffic at weekends, twists as it descends to Nanegalito (Km 56), Miraflores (Km 62), the turn-offs to the old road and to Mindo (Km 79), San Miguel de los Bancos, Pedro Vicente Maldonado and Puerto Quito, before joining the Santo Domingo–Esmeraldas road at La Independencia.

Pululahua ⓘ *US$5*, is a geobotanical reserve in an inhabited, farmed volcanic caldera. A few kilometres beyond the Mitad del Mundo, off the paved road to Calacalí, a lookout on the rim gives a great view, but go in the morning, as the cloud usually descends around 1300. You can go down to the reserve and experience the rich vegetation and warm microclimate inside. From the mirador: walk down 30 minutes to the agricultural zone then turn left. A longer road allows you to drive into the crater via Moraspungo. To walk out this way, starting at the mirador, continue past the village in the crater, turn left and follow the unimproved road up to the rim and back to the main road, a 15-20 km round trip.

Yunguilla ⓘ *T09-114 4610, www.yunguilla.org*, 5 km north of the Calacalí–La Independencia road (turn-off at Km3, opposite the turn for Nono), is a community-run eco-tourism project selling cheese, jam, handicrafts and footballs. It is located at the upper elevation border of Maquipucuna Reserve (see below). It has a cabin (**$$**) with shared bath, full board. Also organizes lodging with families (same price) and camping. Access by pickup from Calacalí US$4, guiding US$25 per day.

In **Nanegalito**, the transport hub for this area is a **tourist information office** ⓘ *T02-211 6222, Mon-Sun 0900-1700*. Just past the centre is the turn-off to Nanegal and the cloud forest in the 18,500-ha **Maquipucuna Biological Reserve**, which contains a tremendous diversity of flora and fauna, including over 325 species of birds. The reserve has eight trails of varying length, from 15 minutes to full day (US$10 per person), totalling 40 km. See Sleeping, below for the lodge. For information: **Fundación Maquipuicuna** ⓘ *www.maqui.org*, which supports reforestation, recuperation of habitats, eg for migratory birds, and aims for a protective corridor linking all areas of the country. Local guides are good and knowledgeable, US$25 (Spanish), US$100 (English) per day for a group of nine.

Next to Maquipucuna is **Santa Lucía** ⓘ *T02-215 7242, www.santaluciaecuador.com*. Access to this reserve is 30 minutes by car from Nanegal. Day tours combining Pululahua, Yunguilla and Santa Lucía are available. Bosque Nublado Santa Lucía is a community-based conservation and eco-tourism project protecting a beautiful 650-ha tract of cloudforest. The area is very rich in birds (there is a cock-of-the-rock lek) and other wildlife. There are waterfalls and walking trails and a lodge (see below).

At Armenia (Km 60), a few km beyond Nanegalito, a road heads northwest through Santa Elena, with a popular handicrafts market on Sunday, to the village and archaeological site of **Tulipe** (14 km; 1450 m). The site consists of several man-made 'pools' linked by water channels. A path leads beside the Río Tulipe in about 15 minutes to a circular pool amid trees. The site **museum** ① *T02-285 0635, www.fonsal.gov.ec, US$2, Wed-Sun 0900-1600, guided tours in Spanish, tip guide*, has exhibits in Spanish on the Yumbos culture and the colonos (contemporary settlers). There is an orchidarium and a restaurant serving trout lunches, US$5. There are other restaurants in Tulipe.

The Yumbos were traders who linked the Quitus and the coastal civilizations between AD 800-1600. Their trails are called *culuncos*, 1 m wide and 3 m deep, covered in vegetation for coolness. Several treks in the area follow them. Also to be seen are *tolas*, raised earth platforms; there are some 1500 in four parishes around Tulipe. **Turismo Comunitario Las Tolas** ① *6 km from Tulipe, T02-286 9488*, offers lodging, food, artesanal workshops and guides to *tolas* and *culuncos*. There are some reserves in the area, see www.cloudforestecuador.com.

Mindo → *Phone code: 02. Regional population: 2900. Altitude: 1250 m.*

Mindo, a small town surrounded by dairy farms and lush cloudforest climbing the western slopes of Pichincha, is the main access for the 19,500-ha Bosque Protector Mindo-Nambillo. The town gets very crowded with Quiteños at weekends and holidays. The reserve, which ranges in altitude from 1400 to 4780 m, features beautiful flora (many orchids and bromeliads), fauna (butterflies, birds including the cock-of-the-rock, golden-headed quetzal and toucan-barbet) and spectacular cloudforest and waterfalls. The region's rich diversity was threatened in 2010 by proposed mining in the area. **Amigos de la Naturaleza de Mindo** ① *1½ blocks from the Parque Central, T217 0115, US$1, guide US$20 for group of 10*, runs the **Centro de Educación Ambiental** (CEA), 4 km from town, within the 17-ha buffer zone, capacity for 25-30 people. Lodging **$** per person, full board including excursion **$$$** per person. Take food if you wish to prepare your own (nice kitchen facilities US$1.50). Arrangements have to be made in advance. During the rainy season, access to the reserve can be rough. Mindo also has orchid gardens and butterfly farms. Activities include visits to waterfalls, with rappelling in the La Isla waterfalls, 'canopy' zip lines, and 'tubing' regattas in the rivers. **Note** There are no ATMs in Mindo, the nearest one is in San Miguel de Los Bancos.

West of Mindo → *Phone code: 02.*

The road continues west beyond the turn-off to Mindo, descending to the subtropical zone north of Santo Domingo de los Tsáchilas. It goes via San Miguel de los Bancos, Pedro Vicente (PV) Maldonado and Puerto Quito (on the lovely Río Caoni) to La Independencia on the Santo Domingo–Esmeraldas road. The entire area is good for birdwatching, swimming in rivers and natural pools, walking, kayaking, or simply relaxing in pleasant natural surroundings. There are many reserves, resorts, lodgings and places to visit along the route, of particular interest to birdwatchers. There are tours from Quito. See Sleeping, below, for resorts.

Around Quito listings

For Sleeping and Eating price codes and other relevant information, see pages 10-11.

● Sleeping

Papallacta *p50*

$$$$ Hotel Termas Papallacta, at the Termas complex, comfortable heated rooms and suites, good expensive restaurant, thermal pools set in a lovely garden, Wi-Fi in computer room, nice lounge with fireplace, some rooms have a private jacuzzi, also cabins for up to 6 (**$$$$**), transport from Quito extra. Guests are provided with identification and can enter any part of the complex and get discounts at the spa. For weekends and holidays book a room at least a month in advance. Recommended.

$$ Antizana, on road to the Termas, a short walk from the complex, T232 0626. Simple rooms, restaurant, cheaper with shared bath, 2 thermal pools, a good option.

$$ La Choza de Don Wilson, at intersection of old unpaved road and road to Termas, T232 0627. Simple rooms with nice views of the valley, includes breakfast, good popular restaurant, hot water, pool, massage, spa run by physiotherapist, very attentive proprietors.

$ Coturpa, next to the Municipal baths in Papallacta town, T232 0640. Restaurant open weekends, hot water, thermal pool and sauna, rooms are functional but very small.

East of Papallacta

$$$ Guango Lodge, near Cuyuja, 9 km east of Papallacta, T02-290 9027 (Quito), www.cabanasanisidro.com. In a 350-ha temperate forest reserve along the Río Papallacta. Includes 3 good meals, nice facilities, excellent birdwatching (grey-breasted mountain toucans are regularly seen here). Day visits cost US$5 per person. Reservations required.

To the western slopes of Pichincha *p50*
Paseo del Quinde

$$$$ Bellavista Cloudforest Reserve, T211 6232 (Bellavista), in Quito at Jorge Washington E7-25 y 6 de Diciembre, T290 1536, www.bellavistacloudforest.com. A dramatic dome-shaped lodge perched in beautiful cloudforest, includes full board (good food, vegetarian on request), 14 rooms with private bath; **$$$** pp in dorm, simple accommodation in research area, also a hill cottage away from main building, camping US$7 pp. Package tours can be arranged including transport from Quito and guide, best booked in advance. Recommended.

$$$$ San Jorge, T339 0403, www.eco-lodge sanjorge.com. A series of reserves with lodges in bird-rich areas. One is 4 km from Quito (see **Hostería San Jorge**, page 31), one in Tandayapa at 1500 m and another in Milpe, off the paved road, at 900 m.

$$$$ Tandayapa Bird Lodge, T244 7520 (Quito), www.tandayapa.com. Designed and owned by birders. Full board, 12 very comfortable rooms with hot water, some rooms have a canopy platform for observation, large common area for socializing, packages available including guide and transport from Quito.

The paved route

$$$$ Maquipucuna Lodge, T02-250 7200, 09-237 1945, www.maqui.org. Comfortable rustic lodge, includes full board with good meals using ingredients from own organic garden (vegetarian and vegan available). Rooms range from shared to rooms with bath, hot water, electricity. Campsite is 20 mins' walk from main lodge, **$** pp (food extra), cooking lessons, chocolate massages, bar.

$$$$ Santa Lucía, T02-215 7242, www.santa luciaecuador.com. The lodge with panoramic views is a 1½-hr walk from the access to the reserve. Price includes full board with good food and guiding. There are cabins with private bath, rooms with shared composting toilets and hot showers and dorms (**$** per person including food but not guiding).

$ Posada del Yumbo, Tulipe, T286 0121. Up a side street off the main road. Large property with cabins with bath and river view, also simple rooms (thin walls), some with bath, electric shower, full board available, pool, horse riding. In same family is restaurant **La Aldea**, beside the archaeologic site.

Mindo *p52*

$$$$ Casa Divina, 1.2 km on the road to Cascada de Nambillo, T09-172 5874, www.mindocasadivina.com. Comfortable 2-storey wooden cabins in a lovely location surrounded by 2.7 forested ha, includes breakfast and dinner, rooms with bathtub, bird-guiding extra, US/Ecuadorean-run.

$$$$ El Carmelo de Mindo, 1 km west of town, T217 0109, Quito T02-222 2837, www.mindo.com.ec. Lodge set in a 32-ha reserve. Rooms, cabins on stilts and tree houses surrounded by nice grounds, price includes full board, walk with a native guide and tubing; river bathing, pool, spa, camping U$10 pp, fishing, horse riding, butterfly farm, cable car, mid-week discounts.

$$$$ El Monte, 2 km form town on road to Mindo Garden, then opposite Mariposas de Mindo, cross river on tarabita (rustic cable car), T217 0102, Quito T02-255 8881, www.ecuadorcloudforest.com. Beautifully constructed lodge in 44-ha property, newer cabins are spacious and very comfortable, lovely bathroom opening onto outside, includes 3 meals, some (but not all) excursions with a native guide and tubing, other adventure sports and horse riding are extra, no electricity, reserve in advance. Recommended.

$$$$ Séptimo Paraíso, 2 km from Calacalí-La Independencia road along Mindo access road, then 500 m right on a small side road, well signed, T09-368 4420, Quito T02-289 3160, www.septimoparaiso.com. All wood lodge in a 420-ha reserve, comfortable, includes breakfast, expensive restaurant, pool and jaccuzi, parking, lovely grounds, great birdwatching, walking trails open to non-guests for US$10. Recommended.

$$$ Caskaffesu, Sixto Durán Ballén (the street leading to the stadium) y Av Quito, T217 0100, caskaffesu@yahoo.com. Pleasant hostal with nice courtyard, includes breakfast, restaurant serves international food, US/Ecuadorean-run.

$$$ El Descanso, 300 m from main street, take 1st right after bridge, T217 0213, www.el descanso.net. Nice house with comfortable rooms, includes breakfast, cheaper in loft with shared bath, ample parking. Recommended.

$$$ Hacienda San Vicente (Yellow House), 500 m south of the plaza, T217 0124, Quito T02-223 6275, www.yellowhousetrails.com. Family-run lodge set in 200 ha of very rich forest, includes excellent breakfast and dinner, nice rooms, good walking trails open to non-guests for US$5, reservations required, good value. Highly recommended for nature lovers.

$$$ Mindo Garden, 3 km form Mindo on road to CEA, T09-733 1092, Quito T02-225 2077, www.mindogardens.com. Comfortable, tastefully decorated cabins in a beautiful setting by the Río Mindo, includes breakfast, restaurant, parking, good birdwatching in 300-ha property.

$ Jardín de los Pájaros, 2 blocks from the main street, 1st right after bridge, T217 0159. Family-run hostel, includes good breakfast, hot water, small pool, parking, large covered terrace, good value. Recommended.

$ Rubby, by the stadium, T09-340 6321, rubbyhostal@yahoo.com. Well maintained hostal with homey feel, includes breakfast, meals on request, cheaper with shared bath, electric shower, nice balcony with hammocks, good value. English spoken, owner Marcelo Arias is a birding guide.

$ Sandy, 1 block from the main street, 1st right after bridge, T217 0212. Family-run hostel in a wooden house, includes breakfast, hot water, nice, good value.

West of Mindo *p52*

$$$$ Arashá, 4 km west of PV Maldonado, Km 121, T02-390 0007, Quito T02-244 9881 for reservations, www.arasharesort.com. Well-run resort and spa with pools, waterfalls (artificial and natural) and hiking trails. Comfortable thatched cabins with good bathrooms, price includes all meals (world-class chef), use of the facilities (spa extra) and tours, can arrange transport from Quito, attentive staff, popular with families, elegant and very upmarket.

$$$ Cocoa, 2 km from Puerto Quito on the road to El Achiote which starts at the town bypass, T02-215 6233, Quito T02-252 9297, www.cocoa.com.ec. Wooden lodge with river views in a tropical fruit growing area, includes full board and guided tours, shared bath, porch with hammocks, trails in the forest leading to waterfalls.

$$$ Selva Virgen, at Km 132, east of Puerto Quito, T02-390 1317, www.selvavirgen.com.ec. Nice *hostería* set in a 100-ha property owned by the Universidad Técnica Equinoccial (UTE). The hotel is staffed by students. Includes breakfast, restaurant, spacious comfortable cabins with a/c, fridge, jacuzzi, and nice porch, cheaper in rooms with ceiling fan, pool, lovely grounds, part of the property is forested and has trails, facilities also open to restaurant patrons.

$$ Suamox, at Km 130, 14 km from PV Maldonado and 10 km from Puerto Quito, T09-944 8741, www.suamoxforest.com. Attractive accommodations in a 110-ha property with native forest and fruit trees, restaurant, cheaper with shared bath, kitchen and laundry facilities, nice atmosphere, good walking and nature observation opportunities in 10 km of trails, reservations required.

$$ Grand Hotel Puerto Quito, along the highway bypass, T02-215 6363, www.granhotel puertoquito.com. Pleasant hotel, restaurant, fan, pool and sauna, parking.

$$ Mirador Río Blanco, San Miguel de los Bancos, main road, at the east end of town, T02-277 0307. Popular hotel/restaurant serving tropical dishes, rooms a bit small, hot water, parking, terrace with bird feeders (many hummingbirds and tanagers) and magnificent views overlooking the river.

🍴 Eating

To the western slopes of Pichincha *p50*
Pululahua
$$$ El Cráter, on the rim of the crater, access right along road to the Mirador, T239 6399, open 1200-1600. Popular upscale restaurant with excellent views. Also has a fancy hotel, www.elcrater.com.

⛰ Activities and tours

To the western slopes of Pichincha *p50*
Pululahua
Horse riding   Green Horse Ranch, Astrid Muller, T08-612 5433, www.horse ranch.de. 1- to 9-day rides, among the options is a 3-day ride to **Bellavista**.

Mindo
Mindo Bird, Sector Saguambi, just out of town on the road to CEA, T217 0188, birdwatching, regattas, cycling, hiking, visits to waterfalls, English spoken, very helpful.
Vinicio Pérez, T09-947 6867, www.bird watchershouse.com, is a recommended birding guide, he speaks some English.

🚌 Transport

Papallacta *p50*
Bus   From **Quito**, buses bound for Tena from Terminal Quitumbe, or buses to Baeza from La Marín, 2 hrs, US$2. The bus stop is east of (below) the village, at the junction of the paved and unpaved roads. A taxi to Termas

costs US$1pp shared or US$3 private. The access to the Termas is uphill from the village along the unpaved road. The complex is a 40-min walk from town. To return to Quito, most buses pass in the afternoon, travelling back at night is not recommended. The Termas also offer van service from their office in Quito and some 5-star hotels, US$110-180 depending on the number of passengers.

Refugio de Vida Silvestre Pasochoa *p50*

Bus From Quito buses run from El Playón to Amaguaña US$0.50 (ask the driver to let you off at the 'Ejido de Amaguaña'); from there follow the signs. It's about 8-km walk, with not much traffic except at weekends, or book a pick-up from Amaguaña, about US$6 for up to 3 people. There is a **Movistar** public phone at the information centre (take a debit card) to call **Cooperativa Pacheco Jr** in Amaguaña, T02-287 7047.

To the western slopes of Pichincha *p50*
Pululahua

Bus Take a 'Mitad del Mundo' bus from La Ofelia Metrobus terminal. When boarding, ask if it goes as far as the Pululahua turn-off (some end their route at Mitad del Mundo, others at the Pululahua Mirador turn-off, others continue to Calacalí). It is a 30-min walk from the turn to the rim.

Tulipe

Bus From **Quito**, Estación La Ofelia, from 0615, US$1.50, 1¾ hrs: **Transportes Otavalo**, 6 daily, continue to Pacto (US$2, 2 hrs) and **Transportes Minas** 4 daily, continue to Chontal (US$2.50, 3 hrs). To **Las Tolas**, **Tranporstres Minas**, daily at 1730, US$2, 2½ hrs or take pick-up from Tulipe, US$5.

Mindo *p52*

Bus From **Quito**, Estación La Ofelia, **Coop Flor del Valle**, T236 4393. Mon-Fri 0800, 0900, 1600, Sat 0740, 0820, 0920, 1600, Sun 0740, 0820, 0920, 1400, 1700. Mindo-Quito: Mon-Fri 0630, 1345, 1500, Sat 0630, 1400, 1530, 1700, Sun 0630, 1400, 1500, 1600, 1700, US$2.50, 2 hrs. Weekend buses fill quickly, buy ahead. You can also take any bus bound for Esmeraldas or San Miguel de los Bancos (see below) and get off at the turn-off for Mindo from where there are taxis until 1930, US$0.50 pp or US$3 without sharing. **Cooperativa Kennedy** to/from **Santo Domingo** 6 daily, US$4, 3½ hrs, 0400 service from Mindo continues to **Guayaquil**, US$9, 9 hrs.

West of Mindo *p52*

From **Quito**, Terminal Carcelén, departures every 30 mins (**Coop Kennedy** and associates) to Santo Domingo via: **Nanegalito** (US$1.50, 1½ hrs), **San Miguel de los Bancos** (US$2.50, 2½ hrs), **Pedro Vicente Maldonado** (US$3, 3 hrs) and **Puerto Quito** (US$3.75, 3½ hrs). **Trans Esmeraldas** frequent departures from Terminal Carcelén and from their own station in La Mariscal, Santa María 870, also serve these destinations along the Quito–Esmeraldas route.

Northern Ecuador

The area north of Quito to the Colombian border is outstandingly beautiful. The landscape is mountainous, with views of the Cotacachi, Imbabura, and Chiles volcanoes, as well as the glacier-covered Cayambe, interspersed with lakes. The region is also renowned for its artesanía.

Quito to Otavalo

On the way from the capital to the main tourist centre in northern Ecuador, the landscape is dominated by the Cayambe volcano.

Quito to Cayambe

Calderón, 32 km north of the centre of Quito, is where the famous bread figurines are made. You can see them being made, though not on Sunday, and prices are lower than in Quito, ranging from about US$0.50 to US$10. On 1-2 November, the graves in the cemetery are decorated with flowers, drinks and food for the dead. The Corpus Christi processions are very colourful. Take a feeder bus at La Ofelia Metrobus terminal.

The Pan-American Highway goes to Guayllabamba where it branches, one road goes through Cayambe and the second through Tabacundo before rejoining at Cajas. At 8 km before Cayambe a globe carved out of rock by the Pan-American Highway is at the spot where the French expedition marked the Equator(small shop sells drinks and snacks). A few metres north is **Quitsato** ① *T02-236 3042, www.quitsato.org*, where studies about the equator and its importance to ancient cultures are carried out. There is a sun dial, 54 m in diameter, and the **Museo de la Cultura Solar** with information about native cultures and archaeological sites along the equator, they have special events for the solstices and equinoxes. At 10 km past Guayllabamba and 8 km before Tabacundo, just north of the toll booth, a cobbled road to the left (signed Pirámides de Cochasquí) leads to Tocachi and further on to the **Tolas de Cochasquí** ① *T02-254 1818, www.pichincha.gov.ec, 0900-1600, US$3, entry only with a 1½-hr guided tour*, archaeological site. The protected area contains 15 truncated clay pyramids, nine with long ramps, built between AD 950 and 1550 by the Cara or Cayambi-Caranqui people. Festivals with dancing at the equinoxes and solstices. There is a site museum and views from the pyramids, south to Quito, are marvellous. From Terminal Carcelén, be sure to take a bus that goes on the Tabacundo road and ask to be let off at the turn-off. From there it's a pleasant 8-km walk; if you arrive at the sign around 0800, you could get a lift from the site workers. A taxi from Tabacundo costs US$12 or US$20 round trip with 1½-hour wait, from Cayambe US$15, US$25 round trip.

Cayambe → *Phone code: 02. Regional population: 60,500.*

Cayambe, on the eastern (right-hand) branch of the highway, 25 km northeast of Guayllabamba, is overshadowed by the snow-capped volcano of the same name. The surrounding countryside consists of a few dairy farms and many flower plantations. The area is noted for its *bizcochos* (biscuits) served with *queso de hoja* (string cheese). At the Centro Cultural Espinoza-Jarrín, is the **Museo de la Ciudad** ① *Rocafuerte y Bolívar, Wed-Sun 0800-1700, free*, with displays about the Cayambi culture and ceramics found at Puntiachil, an important but poorly preserved archaeologic site at the edge of town. There is a fiesta in March for the equinox with plenty of local music; also Inti Raymi during the summer solstice blends into the San Pedro celebrations on 29 June. Market day is Sunday in the traditional plaza up the hill on Calle Rocafuerte.

Volcán Cayambe → *Altitude: 5790 m.*

Cayambe, Ecuador's third highest peak, lies within the **Reserva Ecológica Cayambe-Coca** (US$10). It's the highest point in the world to lie so close to the Equator (3.25 km north), but the equator does go over the mountain's slope. About 1 km south of Cayambe is an unmarked cobbled road heading east via Juan Montalvo, leading in 26 km to the Ruales-Oleas-Berge refuge at 4600 m. The *refugio* costs US$24.40 including tax per person per night, can sleep 37 in bunks; bring a sleeping bag, it is very cold. There is a kitchen, fireplace, running water, electric light and a two-way radio. The standard route, from the west, uses the refuge as a base. There is a crevasse near the summit which can be very difficult to cross if there isn't enough snow, ask the refuge keeper about conditions. There are nice acclimatization hikes around the refuge. Otavalo and Quito operators offer tours here.

Quito to Otavalo listings

For Sleeping and Eating price codes and other relevant information, see pages 10-11.

◉ Sleeping

Cayambe *p57*

Hotels may be full on Fri during Jun-Sep and during the week before Valentine's Day and Mother's Day (high season at the flower plantations).

$$$ Jatun Huasi, Panamericana Norte Km 1.5, T236 3777. US motel style, cabins and rooms with fireplace and frigo-bar, includes breakfast, restaurant, indoor pool, spa, Wi-Fi in restaurant, parking.

$$ Hacienda Guachalá, south of Cayambe on the road to Cangahua, T236 3042, www.guachala.com. A nicely restored colonial hacienda, the chapel (1580) is built on top of an Inca structure. Simple but comfortable rooms in older section and fancier ones in newer area, fireplaces, delicious meals, spring-fed covered swimming pool, Wi-Fi, parking, attentive service, good walking, horses for rent, excursions to nearby pre-Inca ruins, small museum with historical photos.

$$ Shungu Huasi, Camino a Granobles, 1 km northwest of town, T236 1847, www.shungu huasi.com. Comfortable cabins in a 6.5-ha ranch, includes breakfast, excellent Italian restaurant, good hot water supply, Wi-Fi in restaurant, parking, heaters available on request, nice setting, attentive service, offers horse riding and vehicle excursions. Recommended.

$ La Gran Colombia, Panamericana y Calderón, T236 1238. Modern multi-storey building, restaurant, hot water, parking, rooms to the street get traffic noise.

◉ Eating

Cayambe *p57*

$$$ Casa de Fernando, Panamericana Norte Km 1.5. Varied menu, good international food.

$ Aroma, Bolívar 404 y Ascázubi. Large choice of set lunches and à la carte, variety of desserts, very good, open until 2100, Sun until 1800, closed Wed.

⊖ Transport

Cayambe *p57*
Bus Flor del Valle, from La Ofelia, Quito, every 10 mins 0530-2100, US$1.25, 1½ hrs. Their Cayambe station is at Montalvo y Junín. To **Otavalo**, from traffic circle at Bolívar y Av N Jarrín, every 15 mins, US$0.75, 45 mins.

Volcán Cayambe *p58*
Road Most vehicles can go as far as the **Hacienda Piemonte El Hato** (at about 3500 m) from where it is a 3- to 4-hr walk, sometimes longer if heavily laden, or if it is windy, but it is a beautiful walk. Regular pick-ups can often make it to 'la Z', a sharp curve on the road 30-mins' walk to the refugio. 4WDs can often make it to the refugio. Pick-ups can be hired by the market in Cayambe, Junín y Ascázubi, US$35, 1½- 2 hrs. It is difficult to get transport back to Cayambe. A milk truck runs from Cayambe's hospital to the hacienda at 0600, returning between 1700-1900.

Otavalo and around

→ *Phone code: 06. Population: 60,500. Altitude: 2530 m.*

Otavalo, only a short distance from the capital, is a must on any tourist itinerary in Ecuador. The main paved road from Cayambe crosses the *páramo* and suddenly descends into the land of the *Otavaleños*, a thriving, prosperous group, famous for their prodigious production of woollens. The town itself, consisting of rather functional modern buildings, is one of South America's most important centres of ethno-tourism and its enormous Saturday market, featuring a dazzling array of textiles and crafts, is second to none and not to be missed. Men here wear their hair long and plaited under a broad-brimmed hat; they wear white, calf-length trousers and blue ponchos. The women's colourful costumes consist of embroidered blouses, shoulder wraps and many coloured beads. Native families speak Quichua at home, although it is losing some ground to Spanish with the younger generation. Otavalo is set in beautiful countryside, with mountains, lakes and small villages nearby. The area is worth exploring for three or four days.

Ins and outs

Tourist offices Contact iTur ① *corner of Plaza de Ponchos, Jaramillo y Quiroga, T292 7230, Mon-Fri 0830-1300, 1400-1800, Sat 0900-1400, Sun 0900-1200*, for local and regional information. **Cámara de Turismo** ① *Sucre y Quiroga, p2, T292 1994, www.otavaloturismo. com, Mon-Fri 0900-1300*, has information and pamphlets.

Otavalo

The **Saturday market** comprises four different markets in various parts of the town with the central streets filled with vendors. The *artesanías* market is held 0700-1800, based around the Plaza de Ponchos (Plaza Centenario). The livestock section begins at 0500 until 1000, outside town in the Viejo Colegio Agrícola; go west on Colón from the town centre. The produce market lasts from 0700 till 1400, in Plaza 24 de Mayo. The *artesanías* industry is so big that the Plaza de Ponchos is filled with vendors every day of the week. The selection is better on Saturday but prices are a little higher than other days when the atmosphere is more relaxed. Wednesday is also an important market day with more movement than other weekdays. Polite bargaining is appropriate in the market and shops. Otavaleños not only sell goods they weave and sew themselves, but they bring crafts from throughout Ecuador and from Peru and Bolivia. Indigenous people in the market respond better to photography if you buy something first, then ask politely. The **Instituto Otavaleño de Antropología** ① *At Universidad de Otavalo, Av de los Sarances y Pendoneros, 1 block west of the Panamericana Norte, T292 0321, Mon-Thu 0830-1200, 1430-1800, Fri 0830-1200, 1430-1700, free,* has a library, an archaeological museum with

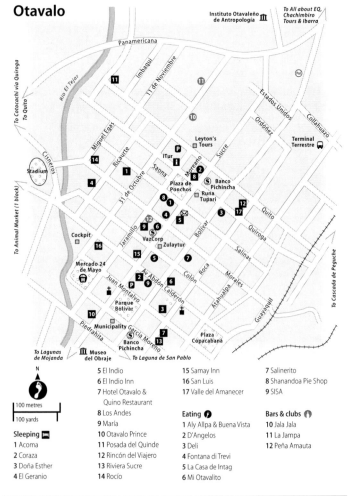

Otavalo

To All about EQ, Chachimbiro Tours & Ibarra

Instituto Otavaleño de Antropología 🏛

Panamericana

To Cotacachi via Quiroga

To Quito

Rio El Tejar

Imbabuqui

11 de Noviembre

Estados Unidos

Collahuazo

Miguel Egas

11

11

Ordóñez

10

Cisneros

Stadium

Ricaurte

Saona

Moreano

Sucre

Terminal Terrestre

Leyton's Tours

14

iTur

1

2

8

31 de Octubre

Banco Pichincha $

To Animal Market (1 block)

4

8

1

Plaza de Ponchos

Runa Tupari

Quito

4

5

12

17

3

Jaramillo

2

9

6

VazCorp

Zulaytur

Bolívar

Quiroga

Cockpit

16

15

5

7

Salinas

To Cascada de Peguche

Mercado 24 de Mayo 🅜

Juan Montalvo

2

9

6

Colón

Roca

Morales

Atahualpa

Guayaquil

Parque Bolívar

3

Piedrahíta

10

Municipality

García Moreno

7

Plaza Copacabana

To Lagunas de Mojanda

🏛 Museo del Obraje

Banco Pichincha $

13

To Laguna de San Pablo

N

100 metres

100 yards

Sleeping 🛏
1 Acoma
2 Coraza
3 Doña Esther
4 El Geranio

5 El Indio
6 El Indio Inn
7 Hotel Otavalo & Quino Restaurant
8 Los Andes
9 María
10 Otavalo Prince
11 Posada del Quinde
12 Rincón del Viajero
13 Riviera Sucre
14 Rocío

15 Samay Inn
16 San Luis
17 Valle del Amanecer

Eating 🍴
1 Aly Allpa & Buena Vista
2 D'Angelos
3 Deli
4 Fontana di Trevi
5 La Casa de Intag
6 Mi Otavalito

7 Salinerito
8 Shanandoa Pie Shop
9 SISA

Bars & clubs 🍸
10 Jala Jala
11 La Jampa
12 Peña Amauta

artefacts from the northern highlands, a collection of musical instruments, and an ethnographic display of regional costumes and traditional activities. **Museo de Tejidos El Obraje** ① *Sucre 6-08 y Olmedo, T292 0261, US$2, Mon-Sat 0900-1200, 1500-1800,* shows the process of traditional Otavalo weaving from shearing to final products.

Around Otavalo

Otavalo weavers come from dozens of communities. In all these villages many families weave and visitors should shop around as the less known families often have better prices. The easiest villages to visit are Ilumán (there are also many felt hatmakers in town and *yachacs*, or shamen, mostly north of the plaza – look for signs); Agato; Carabuela (many homes sell crafts including wool sweaters); Peguche. These villages are only 15-30 minutes away and all have a good bus service; buses leave from the Terminal and stop at Plaza Copacabana (Atahualpa y Montalvo). You can also take a taxi. Allow one to 1½ hours each way.

To reach the lovely **Cascada de Peguche**, from Peguche's plaza, facing the church, head right and continue straight until the road forks. Take the lower fork to the right, but

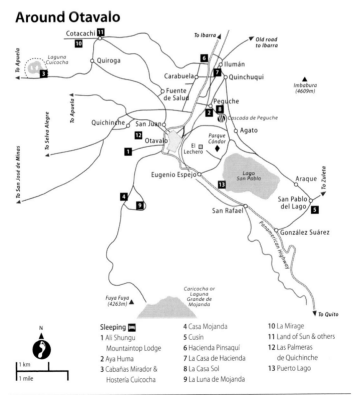

Around Otavalo

Sleeping 🛏	4 Casa Mojanda	10 La Mirage
1 Ali Shungu	5 Cusín	11 Land of Sun & others
Mountaintop Lodge	6 Hacienda Pinsaquí	12 Las Palmeras
2 Aya Huma	7 La Casa de Hacienda	de Quichinche
3 Cabañas Mirador &	8 La Casa Sol	13 Puerto Lago
Hostería Cuicocha	9 La Luna de Mojanda	

not the road that heads downhill. From the top of the falls (left side, excellent views) you can continue the walk to Lago San Pablo. The **Pawkar Raimi** festival is held in Peguche during carnival. At the falls there is a small information centre (contributions are appreciated).

Lago San Pablo
There is a network of old roads and trails between Otavalo and Lago San Pablo, none of which takes more than two hours to explore. It is worth walking either to or back from the lake for the views. Going in a group is recommended for safety. A nice half-day excursion is via Cascada de Peguche, **Parque Cóndor** ① *on a hill called Curiloma, near the community of Pucará Alto, T292 4429, www.parquecondor.org, Tue-Sun 0930-1700, raptor flight demonstrations at 1100, 1500 and 1600, US$3, crowded on weekends*, a reserve and birds of prey rehabilitation centre, and back via **El Lechero**, a lookout by a tree considered sacred among indigenous people. From **San Pablo del Lago** it is possible to climb **Imbabura** volcano (4630 m, frequently under cloud), allow at least six hours to reach the summit and four hours for the descent. An alternative access is from La Esperanza or San Clemente (see page 68). Easier, and no less impressive, is the nearby Cerro Huarmi Imbabura, 3845 m, it is not signed but several paths lead there. Take a good map, food and warm clothing.

Otavalo and around listings

For Sleeping and Eating price codes and other relevant information, see pages 10-11.

🛏 Sleeping

Otavalo *p59, map p60 and p61*
In town
Hotels may be full on Fri night before market.
$$$ Posada del Quinde, Quito y Miguel Egas, T292 0750, www.posadaquinde.com. Nicely decorated hotel with lovely garden, comfortable rooms and suites (**$$$$**), includes breakfast, good restaurant, parking, safe deposit boxes, no smoking. Formerly Ali Shungu, under new management in 2010.
$$ Acoma, Salinas 07-57 y 31 de Octubre, T292 6570, www.hotelacoma.com. Lovely modern hotel built in colonial style, includes breakfast, cafeteria, cheaper with shared bath, parking, nice comfortable rooms, some with balcony, one room with bathtub, 2 suites with kitchenette.
$$ Coraza, Calderón y Sucre, T292 1225, www.hotelcoraza.com. Modern hotel, includes breakfast, good restaurant, Wi-Fi, nice rooms, quiet and comfortable. Recommended.

$$ Doña Esther, Montalvo 4-44 y Bolívar, T292 0739, www.otavalohotel.com. Nicely restored colonial house, restaurant downstairs, sparsely furnished rooms with nice wooden floors, colourful decor.
$$ El Indio Inn, Bolívar 9-04 y Calderón, T292 2922, www.hotelelindioinn.com. Attractive hotel, carpeted rooms and suites, includes breakfast, restaurant, parking, spotless.
$$ Hotel Otavalo, Roca 5-04 y J Montalvo, T292 3712. Refurbished colonial house, includes good breakfast, restaurant offers set meals, large rooms, patio, good service, helpful, a bit pricey.
$ El Indio, Sucre 12-14 y Salinas, near Plaza de Ponchos, T292 0060. In multi-storey building, breakfast, restaurant, hot water, helpful service.
$ Los Andes, Sucre y Quiroga by Plaza de Ponchos, T292 1057. Modern building, cheaper with shared bath, hot water, simple small rooms, good value.
$ Otavalo Prince, Sucre 7-05 y García Moreno, near Parque Bolívar, T292 2540.

Modern hotel, hot water, comfortable rooms, can be a bit noisy at the front.

$ Rincón del Viajero, Roca 11-07 y Quiroga, T292 1741, www.hostalrincondelviajero.com. Very pleasant hostel and meeting place. Simple but nicely decorated rooms, includes a choice of good breakfasts, cheaper with shared bath, hot water, Wi-Fi, laundry facilities, parking, rooftop hammocks and pool table, sitting room with fireplace, camping, US/ Ecuadorean-run, good value. Recommended.

$ Riviera Sucre, García Moreno 380 y Roca, T292 0241, www.rivierasucre.com. Older hotel renovated in 2009, ample rooms, good breakfast, cafeteria, 1 room with shared bath **$**, hot water, laundry facilities, book exchange, nice garden, good meeting place.

$ Rocío, Morales y Egas, T292 0584. Cheaper with shared bath, hot showers, helpful, popular, good value. Also offers cabañas at the edge of town.

$ Samay Inn, Sucre 10-09 y Colón, T292 1826. Nice modern hotel, hot water, small comfortable rooms.

$ San Luis, Abdón Calderón 6-02 y 31 de Octubre, T292 0614. Cheaper with shared bath, hot water, basic, family-run.

$ Valle del Amanecer, Roca y Quiroga, T292 0990, www.hostalvalledelamanecer.com. Small rooms around a nice courtyard, includes breakfast, hot water, popular, bike hire.

$ Camping, in Punyaro, Km 2 vía a Mojanda. US$3 per person, Camping area in a rural property, hot shower and Wi-Fi, arrange through Rincón del Viajero, above.

$ El Geranio, Ricaurte y Morales, T292 0185, hgeranio@hotmail.com. Breakfast available, cheaper with shared bath, electric shower, laundry and cooking facilities, quiet, family-run, helpful, popular, runs trips. Good value, recommended.

$ María, Jaramillo y Colón, T292 0672. Modern multi-storey building, hot water, parking for small car, bright rooms. Very good value, recommended.

Out of town

$$$$ Ali Shungu Mountaintop Lodge, 5 km west of Otavalo by the village of Yambiro, T08-950 9945, www.alishungumountaintop lodge.com. Country inn on a 16-ha private reserve. 4 comfortable nicely decorated guesthouses with capacity for 6, each with living room, woodstove and kitchenette. Includes breakfast and dinner (vegetarian available), horseriding, Wi-Fi, US-run.

$$$$ Casa Mojanda, Vía a Mojanda Km 3.5, T09-972 0890, www.casamojanda.com. Comfortable cabins set in a beautiful hillside. Includes breakfast and tasty dinner prepared with ingredients from own organic garden and short guided hike to waterfall; each room is decorated with its own elegant touch, outdoor hot tub with great views, quiet, good library, horse riding. Recommended.

$$$$ Hacienda Pinsaquí, Panamericana Norte Km 5, 300 m north of the turn-off for Cotacachi, T294 6116, www.hacienda pinsaqui.com. Converted hacienda with 20 suites, one with jacuzzi, includes breakfast, restaurant with lovely dining room, Wi-Fi, lounge with fireplace, beautiful antiques, colonial ambience, gardens, horse riding, biking.

$$$ La Casa de Hacienda, Entrance at Panamericana Norte Km 3, then 300 m east, T269 0245. Tasteful cabins with fireplace, includes breakfast, restaurant serves Ecuadorean and international food, parking, advance reservations required for horse riding.

$$$ Las Palmeras de Quichinche, outside Quichinche, 15 mins by bus from Otavalo, T292 2607, www.laspalmerasinn.com. Cabins and rooms with terrace and fireplace in a rural setting, includes breakfast, restaurant, Wi-Fi, parking, nice grounds and views, pool table and ping-pong, English-owned.

$$ La Luna de Mojanda, On a side road going south off the Mojanda road at Km 4, T09-315 6082. Pleasant country hostel in nice surroundings, some rooms with fireplace and private bath, others shared, cheaper in dorm, terrace with hammocks, pleasant dining room-lounge, restaurant, hot water, parking, camping possible, taxi from Otavalo US$4, bus information on hostel's website, excursions arranged, popular. Recommended.

Around Otavalo *p61, map p61*

$$$ La Casa Sol, near the Cascada de Peguche, T269 0500. Hacienda-style modern hotel built on a hillside. Rooms and suites with balcony, some with fireplace, lovely attention to detail, price includes breakfast and dinner, restaurant.

$$ Aya Huma, on the railway line in Peguche, T269 0164, www.ayahuma.com. In a country setting between the unused rail tracks and the river. Restaurant, hot water, quiet, pleasant atmosphere, live music Sat night, Dutch/Ecuadorean-run, popular. Recommended.

Lago San Pablo *p62, map p61*

$$$$ Cusín, by the village of San Pablo del Lago to the southeast of the lake, T291 8013, www.haciendacusin.com. A converted 17th-century hacienda with lovely courtyard and garden, includes breakfast, fine expensive restaurant, Wi-Fi, 25 rooms with fireplace, sports facilities (pool, horses, bikes, squash court, games room), library, book in advance, British-run. Recommended.

$$$ Puerto Lago, 6 km from Otavalo, just off the Panamericana on the west side of the lake, T292 0920, www.puertolago.com. Modern *hostería* in a lovely setting on the lakeshore, good expensive restaurant overlooking the lake, Wi-Fi, rooms and suites with fireplace, very hospitable, a good place to watch the sunset, includes the use of row-boats, pedalos and kayaks, other water sports extra.

● Eating

Otavalo *p59, map p60*

$$ Fontana di Trevi, Sucre 12-05 y Salinas, 2nd floor. Open 1130-2200. Overlooking C

Sucre, good pizza and pasta, nice juices, friendly service.

$$ Quino, Roca 7-40 y Juan Montalvo, Tue-Sun 1030-2300. Mon 1730-2300. Traditional coastal cooking and some meat dishes, pleasant seating around patio.

$$-$ Buena Vista, Salinas entre Sucre y Jaramillo, www.buenavistaotavalo.com. 1200-2200, Sat from 0800, closed Tue. Bistro with balcony overlooking Plaza de Ponchos. International food, sandwiches, salads, vegetarian options, trout, good coffee, Wi-Fi.

$$-$ Deli, Quiroga 12-18 y Bolívar. Sun-Thu 1100-2000, Fri 1100-2200, Sat 0800-2200. Small place serving good Mexican and international food, also pizza, nice desserts, good value.

$$-$ SISA, Abdón Calderón 4-09 y Sucre. Ecuadorean and international food, à la carte and set meals. Cinema in the same complex.

$ Aly Allpa, Salinas 509 at Plaza de Ponchos. Good-value set meals, breakfast and à la carte including trout, vegetarian, meat. Recommended.

$ D'Angelos, Sucre y Quito. Daily 1000-2200. Very good pizza and lasagna, good service.

$ Mi Otavalito, Sucre y Morales. Good for set lunch and international food à la carte.

Cafés

La Casa de Intag, Colón 465 y Sucre. Mon-Sat 0800-2000, Sun 0900-2000. Fair-trade cafeteria/shop run by Intag coffee growers and artisans associations. Good organic coffee, breakfast, pancakes, salads, sandwiches, sisal crafts, fruit pulp and more.

Salinerito, Bolívar 10-08 y Morales. Daily 0800-2200. Café/deli run by the Salinas de Guaranda coop. Good sanwiches, breakfast, coffee and juices. A good place to buy supplies such as cheese, cold cuts and chocolate.

Shanandoa Pie Shop, Salinas y Jaramillo. 1100-2100, Sat from 0900. Good pies, milk shakes and ice cream, popular meeting place, book exchange.

🎵 Bars and clubs

Otavalo *p59, map p60*
Otavalo is generally safe but avoid deserted areas at night. Nightlife is concentrated at C 31 de Octubre. *Peñas* are open Fri-Sat from 1930, entrance US$3.
Peña Amauta, Morales 5-11 y Jaramillo. Good local bands, welcoming, mainly foreigners.
Jala Jala, 31 de Octubre y Quito. Live dancing music on Fri and Sat night.
La Jampa, 31 de Octubre y Panamericana, www.lajampa.com. Andean and dancing music, popular with Ecuadoreans and foreigners.

⚙ Festivals and events

Otavalo *p59, maps p60 and p61*
The **end of Jun** combines the **Inti Raymi** celebrations of the summer solstice (**21 Jun**), with the **Fiesta de San Juan** (**24 Jun**) and the **Fiesta de San Pedro y San Pablo** (**29 Jun**). These combined festivities are known as **Los San Juanes** and participants are mostly indigenous. Most of the action takes place in the smaller communities surrounding Otavalo, each one celebrates separately on different dates (www.otavaloturismo.com posts schedule), some of them for a full week. The celebration begins with a ritual bath, the Peguche waterfall is used by Otavalo residents (a personal spiritual activity, best carried out without visitors and certainly without cameras). In Otavalo, indigenous families have costume parties, which at times spill over onto the streets. In the San Juan neighbourhood, near the Yanayacu baths, there is a week-long celebration with food, drink and music. **Fiesta del Yamor** and **Colla Raimi 1st 2 weeks of Sep**, feature local dishes, amusement parks, bands in the plaza and sporting events. **Oct Mes de la cultura**, cultural events throughout the month. **30 or 31 Oct Mojanda Arriba** is an annual hike from Quito (2 days) or Malchinguí (1 day)

over Mojanda to reach Otavalo for the foundation celebrations.

⛰ Activities and tours

Otavalo *p59, maps p60 and p61*
Mountain bikes Several tour operators rent bikes and offer cycling tours for US$35-60 a day trip. **Hostal Valle del Amanecer** (see Sleeping), US$8 per day. **La Tierra** craft shop, Salinas 503 y Sucre, Plaza de Ponchos, good equipment. **Taller Ciclo Primaxi**, Atahualpa 2-49 y García Moreno and at the entrance to Peguche, good bikes, US$1 per hr.
Horse riding Several operators offer riding tours. Half-day trips to nearby attractions cost US$20-25. Full-day trips such as Cuicocha or Mojanda, US$35-40.

Tour operators
Most common tours are to native communities, Cuicocha and Mojanda, US$20-30 pp. Independent travel to the Lagunas de Mojanda is not recommended because of public safety problems. Best go with a tour.
All about EQ, Los Corazas 433 y Albarracín, at the north end of town, T292 3633, www.all-about-ecuador.com. Interesting itineraries, trekking and horse riding tours, climbing, cycling, trips to Intag, Piñán, Cayambe, Oyacachi, rafting and kayaking on the Río Intag. English and French spoken, guides carry radios. Recommended.
Chachimbiro Tours, Los Corazas 433 y Albarracín, T292 3633, www.chachimbiro.com. Trips to the Termas Hostería Chachimbiro 1 hr northwest of Otavalo.
Ecomontes, Sucre y Morales, T292 6244, www.ecomontestour.com. A branch of a Quito operator, trekking, climbing, rafting, also sell tours to Cuyabeno and Galápagos.
Leyton's Tours, Quito y Jaramillo, T292 2388. Horseback and bike tours.
Runa Tupari, Sucre y Quiroga, Plaza de Ponchos T292 5985, www.runatupari.com. Arranges indigenous homestays in the

Cotacachi area, also the usual tours, trekking, horse riding and cycling trips.

Zulaytur, Sucre y Colón, p 2, T292 2791. Day trips to artisans' communities, Mojanda, Imbabura, horse riding.

⊖ Transport

Otavalo *p59, maps p60 and p61*
Note Never leave anything in your car or taxi in the street. There are public car parks at Juan Montalvo y Sucre, by Parque Bolívar, and on Quito between 31 de Octubre and Jaramillo.

Bus Terminal at Atahualpa y Ordóñez (no departures after 1830). To **Quito** 2 hrs, US$2, every 10 mins; all depart from the Terminal Carcelén in Quito, **Coop Otavalo** and **Coop Los Lagos** go into Otavalo, buses bound for Ibarra or Tulcán drop you off at the highway, this is not safe at night. From **Quito** by taxi takes 1½ hrs, US$50 one way, US$80 return with 3 hrs' wait; shared taxis with **Taxis Lagos**, www.taxis lagos.com, (in Quito, Asunción 3-82 y Versalles T223 1899; in Otavalo, Roca 8-04, T292 3203) who run a hotel to hotel service (to/from modern Quito only) and will divert to resorts just off the highway; Mon-Sat hourly, 5 departures on Sun, 1½ hrs, US$8.50 pp, buy ticket at least 1 day before, they also go from Quito to Ibarra. Bus to **Ibarra**, every 4 mins, US$0.45, 40 mins. To **Peguche**, city bus on Av Atahualpa, every 10 mins, bus stops in front of the terminal and at Plaza Copacabana, US$0.20. To the **Intag region**, 5 daily.

Lago San Pablo *p62*
Bus From **Otavalo**–San Pablo del Lago every 25 mins, more often on Sat, US$0.25, 30 mins; taxi US$4.

❶ Directory

Otavalo *p59, map p60*
Banks Banco del Austro, Sucre y Quiroga. **Banco del Pacífico**, Bolívar 614 y García Moreno. **Fax Cambios**, Salinas y Sucre, T292 0501, Mon-Sat 0745-1900, poor rates for cash (7 currencies), 3% commission on TCs. **Vaz Corp**, Sucre 11-13 y Morales, T292 3500, Tue-Sat 0830-1700, exchange 8 currencies, 1.8% comission on TCs (minimum US$2). **Internet** Prices about US$1 per hr. Many in town, specially on C Sucre. **Language schools** Instituto Superior de Español, Sucre 11-10 y Morales, p 3, T299 2414, www.instituto-superior.net. **Mundo Andino Internacional**, Salinas 404 y Bolívar, T292 1864, www.mandinospanish school.com. Salsa and cooking classes included. **Otavalo Spanish Institute**, 31 de Octubre 47-64 y Salinas, p 3, T292 1404, www.otavalospanish.com, also offers Quichua lessons. **Post offices** Corner of Plaza de Ponchos, entrance on Sucre, 1st floor, Mon-Fri 0700-1500, Sat 0800-1200.

Cotopaxi, Latacunga & Quilotoa

Cotopaxi and Latacunga

Machachi → *Phone code: 02. Population: 26,000. Altitude: 2900 m.*
In a valley between the summits of Pasochoa, Rumiñahui and Corazón, lies the town of **Machachi**, famous for its horsemen (*chagras*), horse riding trips, mineral water springs and crystal clear swimming pools (open 0800-1530 daily). The water, 'Agua Güitig' or 'Tesalia', is bottled in a plant 4 km from the town and sold throughout the country, plant tours 0800-1200. Annual highland 'rodeo', El Chagra, third week in July; tourist information office on the plaza.

Reserva Ecológica Los Ilinizas
Machachi is a good starting point for a visit to the northern section of the **Reserva Ecológica Los Ilinizas** *US$5*. There is a *refugio*, a shelter below the saddle between the two peaks, at 4740 m, with capacity for 20 and cooking facilities, take a mat and sleeping bag, US$15 per night, camping US$5 per tent (renovated in 2009-2010). Iliniza Norte (5105 m) although not a technical climb, should not be underestimated, a few exposed, rocky sections require utmost caution. Some climbers suggest using a rope and a helmet is recommended if other parties are there because of falling rock; allow two to four hours for the ascent from the refuge, take a compass, it's easy to mistake the descent. Iliniza Sur (5245 m) involves ice climbing despite the deglaciation: full climbing gear and experience are absolutely necessary. Access to the reserve is through a turn-off west of the Panamericana 6 km south of Machachi, then it's 7 km to the village of El Chaupi. A dirt road continues from here 9 km to 'La Virgen' (statue). Nearby are woods where you can camp. El Chaupi hotels arrange for horses with muleteer (US$15 per animal).

Parque Nacional Cotopaxi
ⓘ *Visitors to the park must register at the entrance. Entrance fee: US$10. Park gates are open 0700-1500, although you can stay until 1800. Visitors arriving with guides not authorized by the park are turned back at the gate. The park administration, a small museum (0800-1200, 1300-1700) and the Paja Blanca restaurant and shelter, are 10 km from the park gates, just before Limpio Pungo. (See also Transport section, below.) The museum has a 3D model of the park, information about the volcano and stuffed animals.*

Cotopaxi volcano (5897 m) is at the heart of a much-visited national park. This scenic snow-covered perfect cone is the second highest peak in Ecuador and a very popular climbing destination. Cotopaxi is an active volcano, one of the highest in the world, and its most recent eruption took place in 1904. Volcanic material from former eruptions can be seen strewn about the *páramo* surrounding Cotopaxi; there is a high plateau with a small lake (Laguna Limpio Pungo), a lovely area for walking and admiring the delicate flora, and fauna including wild horses and native bird species such as the Andean lapwing and the Chimborazo Hillstar hummingbird. The lower slopes are clad in planted pine forests, where llamas may be seen.

The **main entrance** to the Parque Nacional Cotopaxi is approached from Chasqui, 25 km south of Machachi, 6 km north of Lasso, and is marked by a Parque Nacional Cotopaxi sign. Once through the national park gates, go past Laguna Limpio Pungo to a fork, where the right branch climbs steeply to a parking lot (4600 m). From here it's a 30-minutes to one-hour walk to the José Ribas refuge, at 4800 m; beware of altitude sickness. Walking from the highway to the refuge takes an entire day or more. The **El Pedregal entrance**, from the northwest, is accessed from Machachi via Santa Ana del Pedregal (21 km from the Panamericana), or from Sangolquí via Rumipamba and the Río Pita Valley. From Pedregal to the refuge car park is 14 km. There are infrequent buses to Pedregal (two a day) then the hike in is shorter but still a couple of hours. The **Ticatilín access** approaches Cotopaxi from the south. From the Panamericana, 1 km north of Lasso, at 'Aglomerados Cotopaxi' (the northern access to Saquisilí) a road goes east to the village of San Ramón and on to Ticatilín (a contribution of US$2 per vehicle may be requested at the barrier here) and Rancho María. Remember to close all gates. From the south, San Ramón is accessed from Mulaló. Beyond Rancho María is a less impacted páramo and the private Albergue Cotopaxi Cara Sur (see below). Walking four hours from here you reach Campo Alto, a tent camp used by climbers. There are other access points from the north, east and south, which go through private land.

Climbing Cotopaxi The ascent from the refuge takes five to eight hours, start climbing at 0100 as the snow deteriorates in the sun. A full moon is both practical and a magical experience. Check out snow conditions with the guardian of the refuge before climbing. The route changes from year to year due to deglaciation. Because of the altitude and weather conditions, Cotopaxi is a serious climb, equipment and experience are required. To maximize your chances of reaching the summit, make sure to be well acclimatized beforehand. Take a guide if you are inexperienced on ice and snow. Agencies in Quito and throughout the Central Highlands offer Cotopaxi climbing trips. Note that some guides encourage tourists to turn back at the first sign of tiredness, don't be pressured, insist on going at your own pace. There is no specific best season to climb Cotopaxi, weather conditions are largely a matter of luck year-round. Just north of Cotopaxi are the peaks of Sincholagua (4873 m), Rumiñahui (4722 m) and Pasochoa (4225 m). To the southeast is Quilindaña (4890 m). The southwest flank has not received as much impact as the west side. There is good walking, and you can climb Morurco (4881 m) as an acclimatization hike. Condors may sometimes be seen. To climb to the summit in one day you have to stay at Campo Alto (see above and Sleeping, below). The route is reported easier and safer than the north face, but a little longer. The last hour goes around the rim of the crater with impressive views.

Lasso → *Phone code: 03. Altitude: 3000 m.*
The railway and the Pan-American Highway cross one another at Lasso, a small town, 33 km south of Alóag. In the surrounding countryside are several *hosterías*, converted country estates, offering accommodation and meals. There are roadside restaurants along the Panamericana.

Latacunga → *Phone code: 03. . Population: 95,000. Altitude: 2800 m.*
The capital of Cotopaxi Province is a place where the abundance of light grey pumice has been artfully employed. Volcán Cotopaxi is much in evidence, though it is 29 km away.

Provided they are not hidden by clouds, which unfortunately is all too often, as many as nine volcanic cones can be seen from Latacunga; try early in the morning. The colonial character of the town has been well preserved. The central plaza, **Parque Vicente León**, is a beautifully maintained garden (locked at night). There are several other gardens in the town including **Parque San Francisco** and **Lago Flores**. **Casa de los Marqueses de Miraflores** ① *Sánchez de Orellana y Abel Echeverría, T280 1382, Mon-Fri 0800-1200, 1400-1800, Sat 0900-1300, free*, in a restored colonial mansion has a modest museum, with exhibits on Mama Negra (see Festivals and events, page 72), colonial art, archaeology, numismatics and a library (free).

Casa de la Cultura ① *Antonia Vela 3-49 y Padre Salcedo T281 3247, Tue-Fri 0800-1200, 1400- 1800, Sat 0800-1500, US$1*, built around the remains of a Jesuit Monastery and the old Monserrat watermill, houses a nice museum with pre-Columbian ceramics, weavings, costumes and models of festival masks; also art gallery, library and theatre. It has week-long festivals with exhibits and concerts for all the local festivities. There is a Saturday **market** on the Plaza de San Sebastián (at Juan Abel Echeverría). Goods for sale include *shigras* (fine stitched, colourful straw bags) and homespun wool and cotton yarn. The produce market, Plaza El Salto has daily trading and larger fairs on Tuesday and Saturday. A tourist **train** runs from Quito to Latacunga, see page 45.

Tourist offices: Cámara de Turismo de Cotopaxi ① *Sánchez de Orellana y Guayaquil, at Plaza de Santo Domingo, T281 4968, Mon-Fri 0800-1200, 1400-1700*, local and regional information, Spanish only. Oficina de Turismo ① *Terminal Terrestre, 2nd floor, Mon-Fri 0900-1200, 1330-1800, Sat 0900-1600, Sun 0900-1400*, staffed by high school students, local and some regional information.

Cotopaxi and Latacunga listings

For Sleeping and Eating price codes and other relevant information, see pages 10-11.

⊖ Sleeping

Machachi *p67*

$$$ Sierra Loma, near Aloasí, 700 m south of Machachi train station, T09-593 8256, www.sierraloma.com. Cabins in the forest for 4, with fireplace, includes breakfast, other meals on requests, camping **$** pp, package with meals, activities and transport from Quito available.

$$$ Chiguac, Los Caras y Colón, 4 blocks east of the main park, T231 0396, amsincholagua@ gmail.com. Nice family-run hostel, comfortable rooms, includes breakfast, other meals available, shared bath, hot water.

$$$ La Estación, 3 km west of the Panamericana, by railway station outside the village of Aloasí, T230 9246, Quito T02-241

3784. Rooms in a lovely old home and newer section, also cabins, fireplaces, meals available (produce from own garden), parking, family-run, hiking access to Volcán Corazón, reserve ahead.

$$$ Papagayo, in Hacienda Bolívia, 500 m west of the Panamericana, turn off just south of the toll booth, T231 0002, www.hosteria-papagayo.com. Nicely refurbished hacienda, pleasant communal areas with fireplace and library, restaurant, cheaper with shared bath, **$** per person in dorm, jacuzzi, internet, laundry facilities, parking, central heating, homey atmosphere, horse riding, biking, tours, popular.

Reserva Ecológica Los Ilinizas *p67*

$$ Chuquirahua Lodge, near the entrance to town, T08-108 1823, T02-223 6607 (Quito), ecuadortreasure@gmail.com. Rustic 2-storey inn, includes breakfast, private bath, **$** pp in dorms for 8, camping US$4 pp, horse riding, trekking and climbing tours, opened in 2010.

$$ Hacienda San José del Chaupi, 3 km southwest of El Chaupi, T09-467 1692, T257 0066 (Quito), haciendasanjosedelchaupi@ yahoo.com. Converted hacienda house and wood cabins in a working farm. Shared rooms for 4 and cabins for 6, includes breakfast, meals available on request, hot water, parking, fireplaces in common areas and cabins, horse riding and rentals, visitors are welcome to participate in farm activities, reforestation with native species, call in advance.

$ La Llovizna, 100 m behind the church, on the way to the mountain, T09-969 9068. Pleasant hostel, sitting room with fireplace, includes breakfast, restaurant, some rooms with bath, hot water, pool table, ping-pong, horse rental.

$ Posada El Chaupi, in front of bus stop, T02-286 0830. Simple family-run hostel, includes breakfast, other meals with family on request, cheaper with shared bath, electric shower, very obliging.

Parque Nacional Cotopaxi *p67*

All these inns are good for acclimatization at altitudes between 3100 and 3800 m. Just below Limpiopungo is the **Paja Blanca** shelter (**$** pp with breakfast, hot water) with 2 very basic huts and a couple of campsites (US$2 per tent, no facilities). The **José Ribas refuge** (entry US$1) has a kitchen, water, and 60 bunks with mattresses; US$24.40 pp per night, bring sleeping bag and mat, also bring padlock or use the luggage deposit, US$2.50.

$$$$ Tambopaxi, 3 km south of the El Pedregal access (1 hr drive from Machachi) or 4 km north of the turn-off for the climbing shelter, T02-222 0242 (Quito), www.tambopaxi.com. Comfortable straw-bale mountain shelter at 3750 m. 3 double rooms and several dorms (**$** pp), duvets, includes breakfast, other meals

available, camping US$7.50 pp, horse riding with advance notice.

$ Albergue Cotopaxi Cara Sur, at the southwestern end of the park, at the end of the Ticatilín road, T08-461 9264 (see Quito, Tour operators), www.cotopaxicarasur.com. Mountain shelter at 4000 m, day use US$1. Total capacity 40, meals available with advance notice, use of kitchen, outhouses, hot shower, sauna, bunk beds (**$** pp) and blankets, transport from Quito and climbing tours available. Campo Alto tent camp (4780 m, US$5 pp) is 4 hrs' walk from the shelter, horse to take gear to Campo Alto US$12, muleteer US$12, equipment rental.

Outside the park

$$$$ San Agustín de Callo, 2 access roads from the Panamericana, 1 just north of the main park access (6.2 km); the 2nd, just north of Lasso (4.3 km), T03-271 9160, Quito T02-290 6157, www.incahacienda.com. Exclusive hacienda, the only place in Ecuador where you can sleep and dine in an Inca building, the northernmost imperial-style Inca structure still standing. Rooms and suites with fireplace and bathtub, includes breakfast and dinner, horse rides, treks, bicycles and fishing. Restaurant (**$$$**) and buildings open to non-guests (US$5-10).

To the southeast of the park lies an area of rugged *páramos* and mountains dropping down to the jungle. The area has several large haciendas which form the **Fundación Páramo**, a private reserve with restricted access.

$$$$ Hacienda Santa Ana, in Santa Ana del Pedregal, T02-222 4950, www.santaana cotopaxi.com. First-class 17th-century former-Jesuit hacienda in beautiful surroundings, 7 comfortable heated rooms, activities on offer include horse riding, biking, trekking, climbing. Opening in late 2010.

$$$$ Hacienda Yanahurco, by Quilindaña, Quito T02-224 1593, www.hacienda

yanahurco.com. Ranch-style rooms with fireplace or heater, includes meals, 2- to 4-day programs, all-inclusive.

$$$ Cuello de Luna, 2 km northwest of the park's main access on a dirt road, T09-970 0330, www.cuellodeluna.com. Comfortable rooms with fireplace, includes breakfast, meals available cheaper in dorm (a very low loft). Can arrange tours to Cotopaxi, horse riding and biking.

$$$ Huagra Corral, 200 m east of Panamericana along the park's main access road, T03-271 9729, www.huagracorral.com. Nicely decorated, includes breakfast, restaurant, some rooms with private bath, portable heaters, convenient location, helpful.

$$$ Tierra del Volcán, T09-972 7934, Quito T02-223 1806, www.tierradelvolcan.com. 3 lodges: **Hacienda El Porvenir,** a working ranch by Rumiñahui, between El Pedregal and the northern access to the park, sitting-room with fireplace, 3 types of rooms, includes breakfast, set meals available, horses and mountain bikes for hire, camping US$3 per person; **Hacienda Santa Rita**, by the Río Pita, on the Sangolquí–El Pedregal road; and the more remote, rustic and economical **Hacienda El Tambo** by Quilindaña, southeast of the park. Also packages including full board and transport from Quito.

Lasso *p68*

$$$$ Hacienda Hato Verde, Panamericana Sur Km 55, by entry to Mulaló, southeast of Lasso, T271 9348, www.haciendahatoverde.com. Lovely old hacienda and working dairy farm near the south flank of Cotopaxi, tastefully restored. 9 rooms with wood-burning stoves, includes breakfast, other meals US$20; activities such as horse riding (for experienced riders), trekking, trip up Cotopaxi Cara Sur, US$80, charming hosts. Recommended.

$$$ Hostería La Ciénega, 2 km south of Lasso, west of the Panamericana, T271 9052, www.hosterialacienega.com. A historic hacienda with nice gardens, an avenue of massive eucalyptus trees, rooms with heater or fireplace, good expensive restaurant.

$$$ San Mateo, 4 km south of Lasso west of the Panamericana, T271 9015, www.hosteriasanmateo.com. Bright rooms and cabañas, pricey restaurant, horse riding included, small but nice, adjoining working hacienda can be visited.

$ Cabañas Los Volcanes, at the south end of Lasso, T271 9524, maexpediciones@yahoo.com. Small hostel, nice rooms, cheaper with shared bath, hot water, laundry facilities, discounts for HI members. Tours to Cotopaxi.

Latacunga *p68*

$$$ Villa de Tacunga, Sanchez de Orellana y Guayaquil, T281 2352, www.villadetacunga.com. Nicely restored colonial house, includes breakfast, restaurant serves set meals and à la carte, Wi-Fi, parking, opened in 2009.

$$ Estambul, Belisario Quevedo 6-46 y Padre Salcedo, T280 0354. Simple quiet hostel long-popular with travellers, cheaper with shared bath, ageing but well maintained although beds are a bit saggy, offer tours to Cotopaxi and Quilotoa.

$$ Makroz, Valencia 8-56 y Quito, T280 0907, hotelmakroz@latinmail.com. Modern hotel with nicely decorated comfortable rooms, restaurant, parking.

$$ Rodelú, Quito 16-31, T280 0956, www.rodelu.com.ec. Comfortable popular hotel, restaurant, nice suites and rooms except for a few which are too small.

$$ Rosim, Quito 16-49 y Padre Salcedo, T280 2172, www.hotelrosim.com. Centrally located, breakfast available, hot water, Wi-Fi, carpeted rooms, quiet and comfortable. Discounts in low season.

$ Central, Sánchez de Orellana y Padre Salcedo, T280 2912. A multi-storey hotel in the centre of town, breakfast available, hot water, a bit faded but very helpful.

$ Tiana, Guayaquil 5-32 y Quito, T281 0147, www.hostaltiana.com. Old house with simple rooms around a stone patio, includes breakfast, nice heated restaurant/café, spotless shared bathrooms, hot water, Wi-Fi, reservations advised for double rooms, **$** pp in dorm. Owners (English and Dutch spoken) have trekking maps, travel information and offer tours. Popular meeting place. Recommended.

🍴 Eating

Machachi *p67*
$$$-$$ Café de la Vaca, 4 km south of town on the Panamericana. Open daily 0800-1730. Very good meals using produce from own farm, very popular.
$$ El Chagra, 3 blocks west of veggie market. Good Ecuadorean food.

Lasso *p68*
You will find several *paradores* (diners) along the Panamericana.

Latacunga *p68*
Few places are open on Sun. Many places on 5 de Junio by Quijano y Ordóñez and along the Panamericana specialize in *chugchucaras*, a traditional pork dish. *Allullas* biscuits and string cheese are sold by the roadside.
$$ Parrilladas La Española, 2 de Mayo 7-175. Mon-Sat 1230-2100. Good grill, popular with locals.
$$-$ Chifa China, Antonia Vela 6-85 y 5 de Junio. Daily 1030-2200. Good Chinese food, large portions.
$$-$ Pizzería Buon Giorno, Sánchez de Orellana y Maldonado. Mon-Sat 1300-2200. Great pizzas and lasagne, large selection. Popular and recommended.
$ Café Colonial, Padre Salcedo 4-62. Set lunches.

Cafés
Coffee Andes Alpes, Guayaquil 6-07 y Quito, by Santo Domingo church. Mon-Sat 1400-2100, Sun 1600-2100. Pleasant café/bar, strong drinks, sweets and sandwiches.

La Fornace, Quito 17-49 y Guayaquil. Daily 1000-2100. Good pizza, coffee, snacks and the best ice cream.

🍷 Bars and clubs

Latacunga *p68*
Galaxy, Barrio El Calvario, on a hill east of the centre. Disco, varied music, nice atmosphere.
Nefertari's, 2 de Mayo 71-45 y Padre Salcedo. Bar, varied music, alternative, rock, salsa, etc.

✳ Festivals and events

Latacunga *p68*
The **La Mama Negra** is held **23-24 Sep**, in homage to the Virgen de las Mercedes. There are 5 main characters in the parade and hundreds of dancers, some representing the black slaves, others the whites. Mama Negra herself (portrayed by a man) is a slave who dared to ask for freedom in colonial times. The colourful costumes are called the **Santísima Trajería**. The civic festival of **Mama Negra**, with similar parade, is on **the 1st or 2nd Sat in Nov** (but not 2 Nov, Día de los Muertos). It is part of the Fiestas de Latacunga, 11 Nov.

🛒 Shopping

Latacunga *p68*
Artesanía Otavalo, Guayaquil 5-50 y Quito. A variety of souvenirs from Otavalo.
Karoma Artesanía: Quito 76-45. A variety of crafts.

⛰ Activities and tours

Latacunga *p68*
All operators offer day trips to **Cotopaxi** and **Quilotoa** (US$40 pp, includes lunch and a visit to a market town if on Thu or Sat, minimum 2 people). Climbing trips to Cotopaxi are around US$170 pp for 2 days (plus park entrance fee and *refugio*), minimum 2 people. Trekking trips US$70-80 pp per day. **Note** Many agencies require passport as deposit when renting gear.

Greivag, Guayaquil y Sánchez de Orellana, Plaza Santo Domingo, L5, T281 0510, www.greivag turismo.com. Cotopaxi and Quilotoa day trips.

Neiges, Guayaquil 6-25, Plaza Santo Domingo, T281 1199, neigestours@hotmail. com. Day trips and climbing.

TribuTrek, at Hostal Tiana, www.tributrek. com. Quality trekking around Quilotoa and Cotopaxi.

Tovar Expediciones, Guayaquil 5-38 y Quito, T281 1333. Climbing and trekking.

⊖ **Transport**

Machachi *p67*

Bus To **Quito**, from C Barriga, 8 blocks south and 2 blocks east of the park – *Especiales* go to Redondel de la Villaflora, Rodrigo de Chávez y Maldonado, south of the colonial city, US$0.75, 1 hr, *Populares* to Terminal Quitumbe, US$0.55. To **Latacunga**, from the monument to El Chagra at the Panamericana, US$0.55, 1 hr.

Reserva Ecológica Los Ilinizas *p67*

Bus From Av Amazonas opposite the market in Machachi, every 30 mins, 0600-1930, to **El Chaupi** (40 min, US$0.36), from where you can walk to the *refugio* in 7-8 hrs. A pick-up from El Chaupi to 'La Virgen' costs US$10, from Machachi US$25. It takes 3 hrs to walk with a full pack from 'La Virgen' to the *refugio*. Horses can be hired at any of the lodgings in El Chaupi.

Parque Nacional Cotopaxi *p67*

Note that only authorized vehicles with a special permit and licensed guide are allowed to take tourists into the park. Others are turned back.

Main park entrance and Refugio Ribas, take a Latacunga bus from Quito and get off at the main access point. Do not take an express bus as you can't get off before Latacunga. At the turn-off to the park there

are usually vehicles from a local operator which go to the park. US$25 to the parking lot before the refuge for up to 3 passengers. From **Machachi**, pickups go via the cobbled road to El Pedregal on to Limpio Pungo and the refugio parking lot, US$35. From **Lasso**, full day trip to the park, US$70 return, contact **Cabañas los Volcanes**. From **Latacunga**, arrange with tour operators or **Hotel Estambul**.

To **Cara Sur** from Quito, **Cotopaxi Cara Sur** offer transport to the **Albergue Cara Sur**, US$60 per vehicle up to 5 passengers. Alternatively take a Latacunga bound bus and get off at **Aglomerados Cotopaxi** and take a pickup from there, US$15 per vehicle for up to 5 passengers.

Latacunga *p68*

Bus Buses leave from the terminal on the Panamericana just south of 5 de Junio, except **Transportes Santa**, which has its own terminal at Eloy Alfaro 28-57 y Vargas Torres, 3 blocks north of the Terminal Terrestre along the Panamericana, T281 1659, serving **Cuenca**, **Loja**, and **Guayaquil** via Riobamba and Pallatanga. To **Quito**, every 15 mins, 2 hrs, US$2; also door to door shared taxis with **Traex Turey**, see page 45. To/from **Ambato**, 1 hr, US$1. To **Guayaquil**, US$7, 7 hrs. To **Saquisilí**, every 20 mins (see below). Through buses, which are more frequent, do not stop at Latacunga Terminal. During the day (0600-1700), they go along a bypass road 4 blocks west of the Terminal, and stop at Puente de San Felipe. At night they stop at the corner of Panamericana and Av 5 de Junio. To **Otavalo**, and **Ibarra**, bypassing Quito, **Cita Express**, hourly from Puente de San Felipe. To **Baños**, every 20 mins from Puente de San Felipe. Buses on the Zumbahua, Quilotoa, Chugchilán, Sigchos circuit are given below. **Note** On Thu most buses to nearby communities leave from Saquisilí market instead of Latacunga.

Latacunga p68

Banks Banco de Guayaquil, Maldonado y Sánchez de Orellana. **Banco Pichincha**, C Quito, Parque Vicente León. **Internet** Prices around US$1 per hr. **Medical services Clínica Latacunga**, Sánchez de Orellana 11-79 y Marqués de Maenza, T281 0260. Private, 24 hrs. **Post office** Belisario Quevedo y Maldonado.

Quilotoa Circuit

The popular and recommended round trip from Latacunga to Pujilí, Zumbahua, Quilotoa crater, Chugchilán, Sigchos, Isinliví, Toacazo, Saquisilí, and back to Latacunga can be done in two to three days by bus (times given below are approximate; buses are often late owing to the rough roads or requests for photo stops). It is 200 km in total. It is also a great route for biking and only a few sections of the loop are cobbled or rough. Access is from either Lasso or Latacunga. Hiking from one town to another can be challenging, especially when the fog rolls in. For these longer walks hiring a guide might not be unreasonable if you don't have a proper map or enough experience.

Latacunga to Zumbahua

A fine paved road leads west to **Pujilí** ⓘ 15 km, bus US$0.25, which has a beautiful church. Good market on Sunday, and a smaller one on Wednesday. Colourful Corpus Christi celebrations. Beyond Pujilí, many interesting crafts are practised by the *indígenas* in the **Tigua** valley: paintings on leather, hand-carved wooden masks and baskets. **Chimbacucho**, also known as Tigua, is home to the Toaquiza family, most famous of the Tigua artists. The road goes on over the Western Cordillera to Zumbahua, La Maná and Quevedo. This is a great downhill bike route. It carries very little traffic and is extremely twisty in parts but is one of the most beautiful routes connecting the highlands with the coast. Beyond Zumbahua are the pretty towns of **Pilaló** (two restaurants and petrol pumps), **Esperanza de El Tingo** (two restaurants and lodging at **Carmita's**, T03-281 4657) and **La Maná**.

Zumbahua

Zumbahua lies 500 m from the main road, 65 km from Pujilí. It has an interesting Saturday market (starts at 0600) for local produce, and some tourist items. Just below the plaza is a shop selling dairy products and cold drinks. Friday nights involve dancing and drinking. Take a fleece, as it can be windy, cold and dusty. There is a good hospital in town, Italian-funded and run. The Saturday trip to Zumbahua market and the Quilotoa crater is one of the best excursions in Ecuador.

Quilotoa

Zumbahua is the point to turn off for a visit to Quilotoa, a volcanic crater filled by a beautiful emerald lake. From the rim of the crater, 3850 m, several snowcapped volcanoes can be seen in the distance. The crater is reached by a paved road which runs north from Zumbahua (about 12 km, three to five hours' walk). Entry fee to Quilotoa US$2. There's a 300-m drop down from the crater rim to the water. The hike down takes about 30 minutes (an hour or more to climb back up). The trail starts to the left of the parking area down a steep, canyon-like cut. You can hire a mule to ride up from the bottom of the crater

(US$7), best arrange before heading down. Take a stick to fend off dogs. There is a basic hostel by the lake and kayaks for rent. Everyone at the crater tries to sell the famous naïve Tigua pictures and carved wooden masks, so expect to be besieged (also by begging children). To hike around the crater rim takes 4½ to six hours in clear weather. Be prepared for sudden changes in the weather, it gets very cold at night and can be foggy.

Chugchilán, Sigchos and Isinliví → *Phone code: 03.*

Chugchilán, a village in one of the most scenic areas of Ecuador, is 22 km by road from the Quilotoa crater. An alternative to the road is a five- to six-hour walk around part of the crater rim, then down to Guayama, and across the canyon (Río Sigüi) to Chugchilán, 11 km. Chugchilán has a woodcarving shop and a cheese factory outside town, and good walking opportunities. Continuing from Chugchilán the road runs through Sigchos, the starting point for the Toachi Valley walk, via Asache to San Francisco de las Pampas (0900 bus daily to Latacunga). There is also a highland road to Las Pampas, with two buses from Sigchos. Southeast of Sigchos is Isinliví, on the old route to Toacazo and Latacunga. It has a fine woodcarving shop and a pre-Inca pucará. Trek to the village of Guantualó, which has a fascinating market on Monday. You can hike to or from Chugchilán (five hours), or from Quilotoa to Isinliví in seven to nine hours. From Sigchos, a paved road leads to Toacazo (**$$ La Quinta Colorada**, T271 6122, price includes breakfast and dinner, very nice) and on to Saquisilí.

Saquisilí → *Phone code: 03.*

Some 16 km southwest of Lasso, and 6 km west of the Panamericana is the small but very important market town of Saquisilí. Its Thursday market (0500-1400) is famous throughout Ecuador for the way in which its seven plazas and some of its streets become jam-packed with people, the great majority of them local *indígenas* with red ponchos and narrow-brimmed felt hats. The best time to visit the market is 0900-1200 (before 0800 for the animal market). Be sure to bargain, as there is a lot of competition. This area has colourful Corpus Christi processions.

Quilotoa Circuit listings

For Sleeping and Eating price codes and other relevant information, see pages 10-11.

⊖ Sleeping

Latacunga to Zumbahua *p74*
Pujilí
$$ El Capulí, García Moreno y Juan Salinas, near the park, T272 4986. Beautifully renovated colonial house, but with an empty feel to it, nice comfortable rooms, includes breakfast, meals on request, Wi-Fi.

Tigua-Chimbacucho
$$ La Posada de Tigua, 3 km east of Tigua-

Chimbacucho, 400 m north of the road, T281 3682, www.laposadadetigua.com. Refurbished hacienda, part of a working dairy ranch, 5 rooms, wood-burning stove, includes tasty home-cooked breakfast and dinner, pleasant family atmosphere, horses for riding, trails, nice views.

Zumbahua *p74*
There are only a few phone lines in town, which are shared among several people. Expect delays when calling to book a room.
$ Cóndor Matzi, overlooking the market area, T08-906 1572 or 03-281 2953 to leave

message. Basic but best in town, shared bath, hot water, dining room with wood stove, kitchen facilities, try to reserve ahead, if closed when you arrive ask at **Restaurante Zumbahua** on the corner of the plaza.

$ Quilotoa, at the north end (bottom) of the plaza, next to the abbatoir, T09-955 2154. Fancy fixtures but a bit run down, hot water, not too clean.

$ Richard, opposite the market on the road in to town, T09-015 5996. Basic shared rooms and one shower with hot water, cooking facilities, parking.

Quilotoa *p74*

$$ Quilotoa Crater Lake Lodge, on the main road facing the access to Quilotoa, T09-794 2123, 12fausto@hotmail.es. Chilly hacienda- style lodge, includes breakfast, restaurant with fireplace and views, new management in 2009.

$ Cabañas Quilotoa, on the access road to the crater, T09-212 5962. Includes breakfast and dinner, cheaper with shared bath, hot water, wood stoves. Owned by Humberto Latacunga, a good painter who will also organize treks.

$ Hostal Pachamama, at the top of the hill by the rim of the crater, T09-212 5962. Includes breakfast and dinner, some rooms with bath, hot water.

Chugchilán *p75*

Note that conventional phones (landlines) were not working in Chugchilán in 2010.

$$$$ Black Sheep Inn, a few mins below the village on the way to Sigchos, T270 8077, www.blacksheepinn.com. A lovely eco-friendly resort which has received several awards. Nice private rooms with wood stoves, includes 3 excellent vegetarian meals, drinking water and hot drinks all day, cheaper with shared bath, **$$** pp in dorm, composting toilets, Wi-Fi extra, library, book exchange, organic garden, sauna, hot tub, gym, waterslide, arrange excursions, discounts for

long stays and cyclists, no credit cards, reservations advised. Highly recommended.

$$ Hostal Cloud Forest, at the entrance to town, 150 m from the centre, T270 8016, josecloudforest@gmail.com. Simple but nice family-run hostel, sitting room with stove, includes dinner (good local fare or vegetarian) and breakfast, cheaper with shared bath, hot water, parking, very helpful owners.

$$ Hostal Mama Hilda, 100 m from centre on the road in to town, T270 8005. Pleasant family-run hostel, warm atmosphere, large rooms some with wood stoves, includes good dinner and breakfast, cheaper with shared bath, **$** pp in dorm, parking, arrange horse riding and walking trips, good value. Highly recommended.

Sigchos *p75*

$ Jardín de los Andes, Ilinizas y Tungurahua, T03-271 2114. Private bath, hot water, parking, basic but quite clean and friendly.

Isinliví *p75*

$$ Llullu Llama, T281 4790, www.llullullama. com. Nicely refurbished house, cosy sitting room with wood stove, tastefully decorated rooms, private, semi-private and dorm (**$** pp), includes good hearty dinner and breakfast, also coffee and tea, shared composting toilet with great views, abundant hot water, organic vegetable garden, warm and relaxing atmosphere, a lovely spot. Recommended.

Saquisilí *p75*

$ Gilocarmelo, by the cemetery, 800 m from town on the road north to Guaytacama, T09-966 9734, T02-340 0924, carlosrlopezc@yahoo.com. Restored hacienda house in a 4-ha property. Plain rooms with fireplace, cheaper in dorm, restaurant, heated pool, sauna, jacuzzi, nice garden.

$ San Carlos, Bolívar opposite the Parque Central. A multi-storey building, electric shower, parking, good value, but watch your valuables. Will hold luggage for US$1 while you visit the market.

⊖ Transport

Zumbahua p74

Bus Many daily on the Latacunga–Quevedo road (0500-1900, US$1.25, 1½ hrs). Buses on Sat are packed full; ride on roof for best views, get your ticket the day before. A pick-up truck can be hired from Zumbahua to **Quilotoa** for US$5-10 depending on number of passengers; also to **Chugchilán** for around US$30. On Sat mornings there are many trucks leaving the Zumbahua market for Chugchilán which pass Quilotoa. Pick-up Quilotoa–Chugchilán US$25.

Taxi Day-trip by taxi to Zumbahua, Quilotoa, return to **Latacunga** is US$40.

Quilotoa p74

Bus From the terminal terrestre in Latacunga **Trans Vivero** daily at 1000, 1130, 1230 and 1330, US$2, 2 hrs. Note that this leaves from Latacunga, not Saquisilí market, even on Thu. Return bus direct to Latacunga at 1300. Buses returning at 1400 and 1500 go only as far as Zumbahua, from where you can catch a Latacunga bound bus at the highway. Also, buses going through Zumbahua bound for Chugchilán will drop you at the turn-off, 5 mins from the crater, where you can also pick them up on their way to Zumbahua and Latacunga.

Chugchilán p75

Bus From **Latacunga**, daily at 1130 (except Thu) via Sigchos, at 1200 via Zumbahua; on Thu from **Saquisilí market** via Sigchos around 1130, US$2.25, 3 hrs. Buses return to Latacunga daily at 0300 via Sigchos, at 0400 via Zumbahua. On Sun there are 2 extra buses to Latacunga leaving 0900-1000. There are extra buses going as far as Zumbahua Wed 0500, Fri 0600 and Sun between 0900-1000; these continue towards the coast. Milk truck to Sigchos around 0800. On Sat also pick-ups going to/from market in Zumbahua and Latacunga. From **Sigchos**, through buses as indicated above, US$0.60, 1 hr. Pickup hire to Sigchos US$25, up to 5 people, US$5 additional person. Pickup to **Quilotoa** US$25, up to 5 people, US$5 additional person. Taxi from Latacunga US$60, from Quito US$100.

Sigchos p75

Bus From **Latacunga** frequent daily service US$1.50, 2 hrs. From/to **Quito** direct service on Fri and Sun, US$3, 3 hrs. To **La Maná** on the road to Quevedo, via Chugchilán, Quilotoa and Zumbahua, Fri at 0500 and Sun at 0830, US$3.50, 6 hrs (returns Sat at 0730 and Sun at 1530). To **Las Pampas**, at 0330 and 1400, US$2.50, 3 hrs. From Las Pampas to **Santo Domingo**, at 0300 and 0600, US$2.50, 3 hrs.

Isinliví p75

From **Latacunga** daily (except Thu), via Sigchos at 1215 (**14 de Octubre**) and direct at 1300 (**Trans Vivero**), on Thu both leave from Saquisilí market around 1100, on Sat the direct bus leaves at 1100 instead of 1300, US$1.80, 2½ hrs. Both buses return to Latacunga 0300-0330, except Wed at 0700 direct, Sun at 1245 direct and Mon at 1400 via Sigchos. Connections to Chugchilán, Quilotoa and Zumbahua can be made in Sigchos. Bus schedules are posted on www.llullullama.com.

Saquisilí p75

Bus Frequent service between **Latacunga** and Saquisilí, US$0.30, 20 mins; many buses daily to/from **Quito** (Quitumbe), 0530-1300, US$2, 2 hrs. Buses and trucks to many outlying villages leave from 1000 onwards. Bus tours from Quito cost US$45 pp, taxis charge US$60, with 2 hrs' wait at market.

Contents

Galápagos Islands

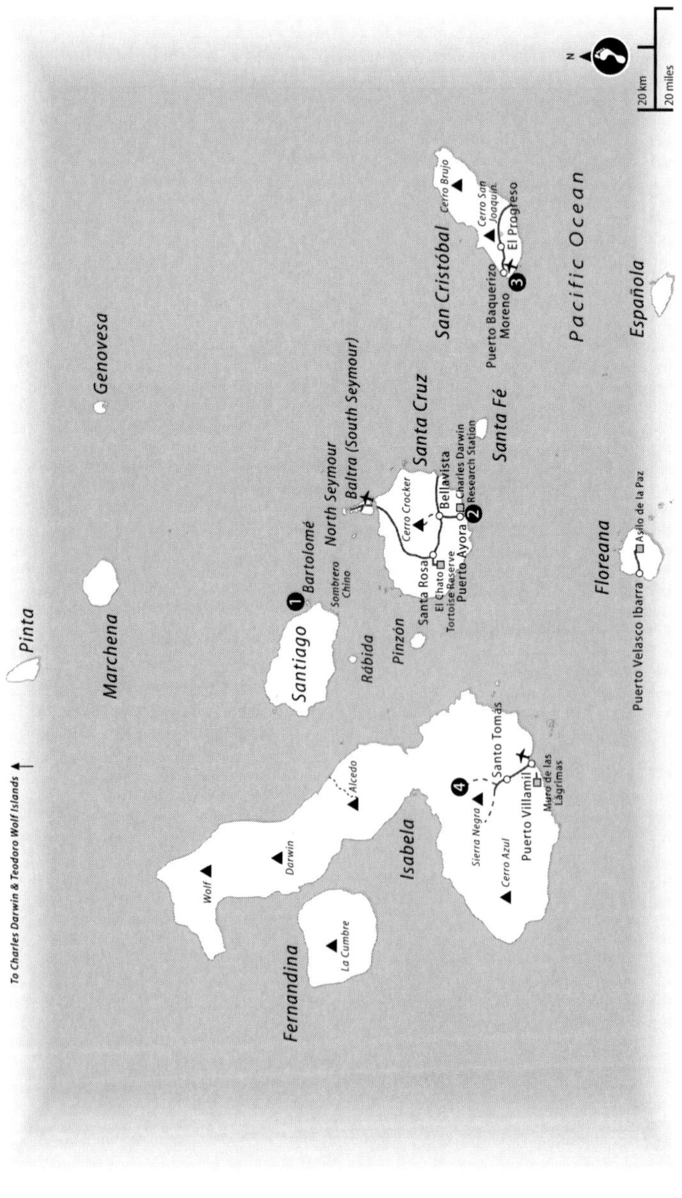
To Charles Darwin & Teodoro Wolf Islands
Pinta
Marchena
Genovesa
Fernandina
La Cumbre
Wolf
Darwin
Alcedo
Isabela
Sierra Negra
Cerro Azul
Puerto Villamil
Santo Tomás
Muro de las Lágrimas
Santiago
Rábida
Pinzón
Sombrero Chino
Bartolomé
North Seymour
Baltra (South Seymour)
Santa Cruz
Cerro Crocker
Santa Rosa
El Chato Tortoise Reserve
Puerto Ayora
Bellavista
Charles Darwin Research Station
Santa Fé
Floreana
Puerto Velasco Ibarra
Asilo de la Paz
San Cristóbal
Puerto Baquerizo Moreno
El Progreso
Cerro San Joaquín
Cerro Brujo
Pacific Ocean
Española
N
20 km
20 miles

Galápagos Islands

A trip to the Galápagos is an unforgettable experience. As Charles Darwin put it: "The Natural History of this archipelago is very remarkable: it seems to be a little world within itself". The islands are world renowned for their fearless wildlife but no amount of hype can prepare the visitor for such a close encounter with nature. Here, you can snorkel with penguins and sea lions, watch 200-kg tortoises lumbering through giant cactus forest, and enjoy the courtship display of the blue-footed booby and frigate bird, all in startling close-up.

A visit to the islands doesn't come cheap. The return flight from Quito and national park fee add up to almost US$500; plus a bare minimum of US$100 per person per day for sailing on an economy-class boat. There are few such inexpensive vessels and even fewer good inexpensive ones. Since you are already spending so much money, it is well worth spending a little more to make sure you sign up with a reputable agency on a better cruise, the quality of which is generally excellent.

Land-based and independent travel on the populated islands are also viable alternatives, but there is at present simply no way to enjoy Galápagos on a shoestring. The once-in-a-lifetime Galápagos experience merits saving for, however, and at the same time, high prices are one way of keeping the number of visitors within sustainable levels. The islands have already suffered the impact of rapidly growing tourism and a mechanism is urgently needed to ensure their survival as the world's foremost wildlife sanctuary.

Background

The Galápagos have never been connected with the continent. Gradually, over many hundreds of thousands of years, animals and plants from over the sea somehow migrated there and as time went by they adapted themselves to Galápagos conditions and came to differ more and more from their continental ancestors. Unique marine and terrestrial environments, due to the continuing volcanic formation of the islands in the west of the archipelago and its location at the nexus of several major marine currents, has created laboratory-type conditions where only certain species have been allowed access. The formidable barriers which prevent many species from travelling within the islands, has led to a very high level of endemism. A quarter of the species of shore fish, half of the plants and almost all the reptiles are found nowhere else. In many cases different forms have evolved on the different islands. Charles Darwin recognized this speciation within the archipelago when he visited the Galápagos on the *Beagle* in 1835 and his observations played a substantial part in his formulation of the theory of evolution.

This natural experiment has been under threat ever since the arrival of the first whaling ships and even more so since the first permanent human settlement. New species were introduced and spread very rapidly, placing the endemic species at risk. Quarantine programmes have since been implemented in an attempt to prevent the introduction and spread of even more species, but the rules are not easy to enforce. There have also been campaigns to eradicate some of the introduced species on some islands, but this is inevitably a very slow, expensive and difficult process.

One extraordinary feature of the islands is the tameness of the animals. The islands were uninhabited when they were discovered in 1535 and the animals still have little instinctive fear of man.

Plant and animal species are grouped into three categories. **Endemic species** are those which occur only in the Galápagos and nowhere else on the planet. Examples of **Galápagos endemics** are the Galápagos marine and Galápagos land iguana, Galápagos fur sea lion, flightless cormorant and the 'daisy tree' (*Scalesia pedunculata*). **Native species** make their homes in the Galápagos as well as other parts of the world. Examples include all three species of boobies, frigate birds and the various types of mangroves. Although not unique to the islands, these native species have been an integral part of the Galápagos ecosystems for a very long time. **Introduced species** on the other hand are very recent arrivals, brought by man, and inevitably the cause of much damage. They include cattle, goats, donkeys, pigs, dogs, cats, rats and over 500 species of plant such as elephant grass (for grazing cattle), and fruit trees. The unchecked expansion of these introduced species has upset the natural balance of the archipelago. The number of tourists also has grown steadily: from 11,800 in 1979, to 68,900 in 2000, to 163,000 in 2009. In July 2007, as a result of the pressures that accompany human activity, the Galápagos were placed on the UNESCO list of endangered World Heritage Sites. Thanks to efforts to control the situation and a decrease in the number of visitors in 2009-2010, it was removed from this list in July 2010.

Ins and outs → *Phone code: 05. For listings, see pages 92-97.*

Getting there

Air There are two airports which receive flights from mainland Ecuador, but no international flights to Galápagos. The most frequently used airport is at **Baltra**, across a narrow strait from Santa Cruz, the other at **Puerto Baquerizo Moreno**, on San Cristóbal. The two islands are 96 km apart and on most days there are local flights in light aircraft between them, as well as to **Puerto Villamil** on Isabela. There is also boat service between Puerto Ayora, Puerto Baquerizo Moreno, Puerto Villamil and occasionally Floreana.

TAME has two daily flights from Quito to Baltra, one stops on route in Guayaquil. TAME also operates Monday, Wednesday, Friday and Saturday to San Cristóbal. **AeroGal** likewise flies twice daily to Baltra, and daily to San Cristóbal. **LAN** is scheduled to begin flights to Baltra in late 2010. The return fare in high season is US$423 from Quito, US$373 from Guayaquil. The low season fare (1 May-14 June, 15 September-31 October) is US$367 from Quito, US$329 from Guayaquil. The same prices apply regardless of whether you fly to San Cristóbal or Baltra; you can arrive at one and return from the other. You can also depart from Quito and return to Guayaquil or vice versa, but you may not buy a one-way ticket. The above prices are subject to change without notice. Discount fares for Ecuadorean nationals and residents of Galápagos are not available to foreigners and these rules are strictly enforced. A 15% discount off the high season fare is available to students with an ISIC card.

Airport transfer Two buses meet flights from the mainland at Baltra: one runs to the port or *muelle* (10 minutes, no charge) where the cruise boats wait; the other goes to Canal de Itabaca, the narrow channel which separates Baltra from Santa Cruz. It is 15 minutes to the Canal, free, then you cross on a small ferry for US$1, another bus waits on the Santa Cruz side to take you to Puerto Ayora in 45 minutes, U$2. If you arrive at Baltra on one of the local inter-island flights (see below) then you have to wait until the next flight from the mainland for bus service, or hire two pickup trucks and a motorboat at the canal (total US$25). For the return trip to the airport, two buses per flight leave Puerto Ayora from the **Terminal Terrestre** on Avenida Baltra, 2 km from the pier. A kiosk near the pier sells bus tickets to the airport but it is seldom open, best to confirm details locally with your airline. Pickup truck from town to bus station, US$1. ⏵ *See also Transport, page 97.*

Getting around

Emetebe Avionetas ① *Guayaquil T04-229 2492, www.emetebe.com, see Directory for local offices,* offers inter-island flights in two light twin-engine aircraft. Two daily flights operate between **Puerto Baquerizo Moreno** (San Cristóbal), **Baltra** and **Puerto Villamil** (Isabela), most days except Sunday, but this varies with passenger demand. Baggage allowance 25 lbs, strictly enforced. All fares US$158 one way, US$263 return, including taxes.

Fibras (fibreglass motor launches for about 15 passengers) operate daily between Puerto Ayora and Puerto Baquerizo Moreno, 2½ hours, and between Puerto Ayora and Puerto Villamil, three hours. They charge US$30, one way. The *fibras* leave Puerto Baquerizo Moreno and Puerto Villamil early each morning and return from Puerto Ayora around 1400. Tickets are sold by several agencies in Puerto Baquerizo Moreno, at the pier in Puerto Ayora, and across the street from the police station in Puerto Villamil. This can be a wild wet ride, life vests are supposed to be carried but check. Take sun protection, your own drinking water, and avoid single-engine boats.

Information and advice

A recommended web site is **www.galapagospark.org**. It describes each visitor site and gives details of guides and tourist vessels operating in the islands.

Tourist offices Santa Cruz (Puerto Ayora): Ministerio de Turismo ① *Av Charles Darwin y Tomás de Berlanga, T252 6174, Mon-Fri 0800-1230, 1400-1730*. **iTur** (Dirección Municipal de Turismo) ① *at the bus terminal, 2 km from town, daily 1000-1700, and another at Baltra airport, www.santacruz.gov.ec*, has information about Puerto Ayora and Santa Cruz Island. **CAPTURGAL** ① *Galápagos Chamber of Tourism, Av Charles Darwin y Charles Binford, T252 6206, www.galapagostour.org, Mon-Fri 0730-1200, 1400-1730*, English spoken. This is the place to present any serious complaints about cruise vessels, agencies or other tourist services. **San Cristóbal** (Puerto Baquerizo Moreno): **CATURCRIST** ① *Hernández y 12 de Febrero, T252 0592, ctcsancrist@easynet.net.ec, Mon-Fri 0730-1230, 1400-1700*, is the San Cristóbal Chamber of Tourism. **Municipal tourist office** ① *Malecón Charles Darwin y 12 de Febrero, T252 1166, Mon-Fri 0730-1230, 1400-1700*, is at the Municipio.

Entry fees On arrival, every foreign visitor to Galápagos must pay a **US$100 National Park fee** plus an additional **US$10 INGALA fee**, both cash only. Be sure to have your passport to hand at the airport and keep all fee receipts throughout your stay in the islands.

Basic rules Do not touch any of the animals, birds or plants. Do not transfer sand, seeds or soil from one island to another. Do not leave litter anywhere; nor take food on to the islands. Do not take anything off the islands. Uninhabited islands are no-smoking zones.

What to take A remedy for seasickness is recommended; the waters south of Santa Cruz are particularly choppy. A good supply of sun block and skin cream to prevent windburn and chapped lips is essential, as are a hat and sunglasses. You should be prepared for dry and wet landings, the latter involving wading ashore. Take plenty of memory cards or film with you; the animals are so tame that you will use far more than you expected; a telephoto lens is not essential, but if you have one, bring it. Also take filters suitable for strong sunlight. Snorkelling equipment is particularly useful as much of the sea-life is only visible under water. Most of the cheaper boats do not provide equipment and those that do may not have good snorkelling gear. If in doubt, bring your own, rent in Puerto Ayora, or buy it in Quito. Always bring some US dollars cash to Galápagos. There is only one bank and ATM system, which may not work with all cards.

Tipping A ship's crew and guides are usually tipped separately. The amount is a very personal matter; you may be guided by suggestions made onboard or in the agency's brochures, but the key factors should always be the quality of service received and your own resources.

If you have problems Raise any issues first with your guide or ship's captain. Additional complaints may be made to **CAPTURGAL** in Puerto Ayora, see above.

Best time to visit The Galápagos climate can be divided into a hot season (December-May), when there is a possibility of heavy showers, and the cool or *garúa* (mist) season (June-November), when the days generally are more cloudy and there is often rain or drizzle. July and August can be windy, Force 4 or 5. Daytime clothing should be lightweight. (Clothing generally, even on 'luxury cruises', should be casual and comfortable.) At night, however, particularly at sea and at higher altitudes, temperatures fall below 15°C and warm clothing is required. Boots and shoes soon wear out on the lava terrain. The sea is cold July-October; underwater visibility is best January-March. Ocean temperatures are usually higher to the east and lower at the western end of the archipelago. The islands climate and hence its wildlife are also influenced by the El Niño phenomenon. Despite all these variations, conditions are generally favourable for visiting Galápagos throughout the year.

The authorities At least six different authorities have a say in running the Galápagos Islands and surrounding marine reserve: 1) **Instituto Nacional Galápagos** (INGALA), under control of the president of Ecuador, which issues residency permits; 2) the **National Park Service**, under the authority of the Ministerio del Ambiente, which regulates tourism and manages the 97% of the archipelago which is parkland; 3) the **Charles Darwin Research Station** (www.darwinfoundation .org), part of an international non-profit organization which supports scientific research, advises other authorities regarding conservation, and channels funds for this purpose; 4) the **Ecuadorean Navy**, which patrols the waters of the archipelago and attempts to enforce regulations regarding both tourism and fishing; 5) **SICGAL**, in charge of controlling movement of live animals, plants and many foods including fresh fruit, vegetables and dairy products (all forbidden). They check bags at Quito and Guayaquil airport, and also when travelling independently between islands. 6) local **elected authorities** including municipalities, the provincial council, and a member of the national Congress. There are also various other **international NGOs** working in Galápagos, each with its own agenda.

Choosing a tour
There are two ways to travel around the islands: a cruise (*tour navegable*), where you sleep on the boat, or shore-based tours on which you take day trips to the islands. On the former you travel at night, arriving at a new landing site each day, with more time ashore. Cruises are for three, four, seven or 14 nights. On a land-based tour you spend less time ashore at wildlife sites, cover less ground and cannot visit the more distant islands. Itineraries are controlled by the National Park to distribute tourism evenly throughout the islands. A third option is independent travel on the populated islands. Although neither cheap nor a substitute for either of the above, it allows those with plenty of time to explore a small part of the archipelago at their leisure. If taking a day trip by boat (*tour diario*), you should check with one of the information offices if a boat is authorized for such trips; many are not. All tours begin with a morning flight from the mainland on the first day and end on the last day with a midday flight back to the mainland.

The less expensive boats are normally smaller and less powerful so you see less and spend more time travelling; also the guiding may be mostly in Spanish. The more expensive boats will probably have air conditioning, hot water and private baths. All boats have to conform to certain minimum safety standards; more expensive boats are better equipped. A water maker can be a great asset. Note that boats with over 20 passengers take quite a time to disembark and re-embark people, while the smaller boats have a more lively motion, which is important if you are prone to seasickness. Note also that there may be limitations for vegetarians on the cheaper boats, enquire in advance. The least expensive boats (economy class) cost about US$175 per person per day and a few of these vessels are dodgy. For around US$200-300 per day (tourist and tourist superior class) you will be on a better, faster boat which can travel more quickly between visitor sites, leaving more time to spend ashore. Over US$350 per day are the first-class and luxury brackets, with far more comfortable and spacious cabins, as well as a superior level of service and cuisine. No boat may sail without a park-trained guide. There are three levels of guides, with level three being the most advanced. A list of guides, their level and languages spoken is found in the National Park website, www.galapagospark.org. For a list of tourist boats, visit www.ecuador-travel.net. Captains, crews and guides regularly change on all boats. These factors, as well as the sea, weather and your fellow passengers will all influence the quality of your experience.

Note Over the years, we have received repeated serious complaints about the vessel *Free Enterprise*, sometimes also called *Intrepid* or *Discovery*. The *Gaby* (also known as *Friendship*) has likewise received negative reports.

Booking a tour in advance You can book a Galápagos cruise in several different ways: 1) over the internet; 2) from either a travel agency or directly though a Galápagos wholesaler in your home country; 3) from one of the very many agencies found throughout Ecuador, especially in Quito but also in other tourist centres and Guayaquil; or 4) from agencies in Puerto Ayora but not Puerto Baquerizo Moreno. The trade-off is always between time and money: booking from home is most efficient and expensive, Puerto Ayora cheapest and most time-consuming, while Quito and Guayaquil are intermediate. Prices for a given category of boat do not vary all that much however, and it is not possible to obtain discounts or make last-minute arrangements in high season. When looking for a last-minute cruise in Puerto Ayora it is best to pay your hotel one night at a time since hoteliers may not refund advance payments. Especially on cheaper boats, check carefully about what is and is not included (eg drinking water, snorkelling equipment, etc).

Cruising It is possible but expensive to cruise the islands in your own yacht. The same rules apply regarding national park fees and being accompanied by a park-trained guide. See under Puerto Ayora, Directory (page 97), for agents who can help organize logistics, paperwork and cruises on local vessels.

The islands

Lying on the Equator, 970 km west of the Ecuadorean coast, the Galápagos consist of six main islands (San Cristóbal, Santa Cruz, Isabela, Floreana, Santiago and Fernandina – the last two uninhabited), 12 smaller islands (Baltra and the uninhabited islands of Santa Fe, Pinzón, Española, Rábida, Daphne, Seymour, Genovesa, Marchena, Pinta, Darwin and Wolf) and over 40 islets. The islands have an estimated population of almost 31,000, but this does not include temporary inhabitants. The largest island, Isabela (formerly Albemarle), is 120 km long and forms half the total land area of the archipelago. Its notorious convict colony was closed in 1959; some 2600 people live there now, mostly in and around Puerto Villamil, on the south coast. San Cristóbal (Chatham) has a population of 7100 with the capital of the archipelago, Puerto Baquerizo Moreno. Santa Cruz (Indefatigable) has 21,000, with Puerto Ayora the main tourist centre; and Floreana (Charles) about 100.

Santa Cruz: Puerto Ayora → *Phone code: 05. Population: 18,000.*

Santa Cruz is the most central of the Galápagos islands and the main town is Puerto Ayora. About 1.5 km from Puerto Ayora is the **Charles Darwin Research Station** ① *Academy Bay, office Mon-Fri 0700-1600, visitor areas 0600-1800 daily.* A visit to the station is a good introduction to the islands as it provides a lot of information. Collections of several of the rare sub-species of giant tortoise are maintained on the station as breeding nuclei, together with tortoise-rearing pens for the young. See www.darwinfoundation.org for more information.

One of the most beautiful beaches in the Galápagos Islands is at **Tortuga Bay**, 45 minutes easy walk (2.5 km each way) west from Puerto Ayora on an excellent cobbled path through cactus forest. Start at the west end of Calle Charles Binford; further on there is a gate where you must register, open 0600-1800 daily, free. Make sure you take sun screen, drinking water, and beware of the very strong undertow. Also, do not walk on the dunes above the beach, which are a marine tortoise nesting area. Ten minutes' walk to the west end of Tortuga Bay is a trail to a lovely mangrove-fringed lagoon, with calmer and warmer water and shade under the mangroves.

Las Grietas is a beautiful gorge with a pool at the bottom which is splendid for bathing. Take a water taxi from the port to the dock at Punta Estrada (five minutes, US$0.50). It is a five-minute walk from here to the *Finch Bay* hotel and 15 minutes further over rough lava boulders to Las Grietas – well worth the trip. The highest point on Santa Cruz Island is **Cerro Crocker**, at 864 m. You can hike here and to two other nearby 'peaks' called **Media Luna** and **Puntudo**. The trail starts at Bellavista (7 km from Puerto Ayora) where a rough trail map is painted as a mural on the wall of the school. The round trip from Bellavista takes six to eight hours. A permit and guide are not required, but a guide may be helpful. Always take food, water and a compass or GPS.

There are a number of sites worth visiting in the interior, including **Los Gemelos**, a pair of twin sinkholes, formed by a collapse of the ground above a fault. They straddle the road to Baltra, beyond Santa Rosa. You can take a *camioneta* all the way, otherwise take a bus to Santa Rosa (see below), then walk. It's a good place to see the Galápagos hawk and barn owl. There are several **lava tubes** (natural tunnels) on the island. Some are at **El Mirador**, 3 km from Puerto Ayora on the road to Bellavista. Two more lava tubes are 1 km from Bellavista. They are on private land, it costs US$1.50 to enter the tunnels (bring a torch) and it takes about 30 minutes to walk through the tunnels. Tours to the lava tubes can be arranged in Puerto Ayora.

Another worthwhile trip is to the **El Chato Tortoise Reserve**, where giant tortoises can be seen in the wild during the dry season. The trail starts at Santa Rosa, 22 km from Puerto Ayora. Past the school in Santa Rosa, a Parque Nacional Galápagos sign warns that tourists have been lost along the trail. Turn left here and follow a badly overgrown path south between two barbed wire fences. After 3 km you reach a wooden memorial to an Israeli tourist and a better trail running east-west. Turn right and follow the trail west for 20 minutes to a sign, "Entrada Al Chato". There are many confusing trails in the reserve itself; take food, water and a compass or GPS. The round trip on foot takes a full day, or horses can sometimes be hired at Santa Rosa. It is best to take a guide if you have no hiking experience; tours can also be arranged in Puerto Ayora.

Near the reserve is the **Butterfly Ranch** (Hacienda Mariposa) ① *US$2, camping possible for US$10-15 pp*, where you can see giant tortoises in the pastures, but only in the dry season. In the wet season the tortoises are breeding down in the arid zone. The ranch is beyond Bellavista on the road to Santa Rosa (the bus passes the turn-off, walk 1 km from there).

San Cristóbal: Puerto Baquerizo Moreno → *Phone code: 05. Population: 7100.*

Puerto Baquerizo Moreno, on San Cristóbal island to the east, is the capital of the archipelago. It is a pleasant place to spend a few days, with interesting excursions in the area. The town's attractive *malecón* has a tidepool with a water shute, a fountain with a 3-D map of the islands and many shaded seats.

In town, the **cathedral** ① *on Av Northía, 2 blocks up from the post office, 0900-1200, 1600-1800*, has interesting artwork combining religious and Galápagos motifs. To the north of town, opposite Playa Mann, is the Galápagos National Park visitor centre or **Centro de Interpretación** ① *T252 0138, ext 102, daily 0700-1700, free.* It has an excellent display of the natural and human history of the islands.

A good trail goes from the Centro de Interpretación to the northeast through scrub forest to **Cerro Tijeretas**, a hill overlooking town and the ocean, 30 minutes away (take water). Side trails branch off to lookouts on cliffs over the sea. Frigatebirds nest in this area and can be observed gliding about, there are sea lions on the beaches below. To go back, if you take the trail which follows the coast, you will end up at **Playa Punta Carola**, a popular surfing beach, too rough for swimming. Closer to town is the small **Playa Mann** (follow Avenida Northía to the north), more suited for swimming, and in town is **Playa de Oro**, where some hotels are located. Right in the centre of town, along the sand by the tidal pool, sea lions can be seen, be careful with the male who 'owns' the beach. To the south of town, 20 minutes' walk past the airport, is **La Lobería**, a rocky bay with shore birds, sea lions and Marine Iguanas.

Around San Cristóbal There are five buses a day inland from Puerto Baquerizo Moreno to **El Progreso** (6 km, 15 minutes, US$0.20), then it's a 2½-hour walk to El Junco lake, the largest body of fresh water in Galápagos. There are also frequent pick-up trucks to El Progreso (US$2), or you can hire a pickup in Puerto Baquerizo Moreno for touring: US$18 to El Junco, US$30 continuing to the beaches at Puerto Chino on the other side of the island, past a man-made tortoise reserve. Prices are return and include waiting. At El Junco there is a path to walk around the lake in 20 minutes. The views are lovely in clear weather but it is cool and wet in the *garúa* season, so take adequate clothing. Various small roads fan out from El Progreso and make for pleasant walking. **Jatun Sacha** (www.jatunsacha.org) has a volunteer centre on an old hacienda in the highlands beyond El Progreso working on eradication of invasive species and a native plants nursery (US$15 taxi ride from town), take repellent.

It's a three-hour hike from the landing site at **Caleta Tortuga**, on the northwest shore of the island, to **La Galapaguera Natural** where you can see tortoises in the wild.

Isla Lobos is an islet with a large sea lion colony and nesting site for sea birds northeast of Puerto Baquerizo Moreno. It is also a dive site.

Boats go to **Puerto Ochoa**, 15 minutes, for the beach and to **Punta Pitt** in the far north where you can see all three species of booby (US$65 for tour). Off the northwest coast is **Kicker Rock** (León Dormido), the basalt remains of a crater; many seabirds, including Nazca and blue-footed boobies, can be seen around its cliffs (five hour trip, including snorkelling, recommended, US$35).

Note: Always take food, plenty of water and a compass or GPS when hiking on your own on San Cristóbal. There are many crisscrossing animal trails and it is easy to get lost. Also watch out for the large-spined opuntia cactus and the poisonwood tree (*manzanillo*), which is a relative of poison ivy and can cause severe skin reactions.

Isabela Island: Puerto Villamil → *Phone code: 05. Population 2600.*

This is the largest island in the archipelago, formed by the extensive lava flows from six volcanoes. Five of the volcanoes are active and each has (or had) its own separate sub-species of giant tortoise. Isabela is developing for land-based tourism. If you have a few days to spare and are looking for tranquillity in a South-Pacific-island setting, this may be just the place. Most residents live in **Puerto Villamil** (population 2500). In the highlands, there is a cluster of farms at Santo Tomás. There are several lovely beaches right by town, but mind the strong undertow and ask locally about the best spots for swimming. It is 2½ hours' walk west to **Muro de las Lágrimas**, a gruesome place built by convict labour under hideous conditions. Along the same road 30 minutes from town is the **Centro de Crianza**, a breeding centre for giant tortoises surrounded by lagoons with flamingos and other birds. In the opposite direction, 30 minutes east toward the *embarcadero* (fishing pier) is **Concha Perla Lagoon**, with a nice access trail through mangroves and a little dock from which you can go swimming with sea lions and other creatures. Fishermen can take you to **Las Tintoreras** a set of small islets in the harbour where white-tipped reef sharks may be seen in the still crystalline water (US$20 per person for a three-hour tour). **Sierra Negra Volcano** has the largest basaltic caldera in the world, 9 x 10 km. It is 19 km (30 minutes) by pickup truck to the park entrance (take passport and National Park entry receipt), where you switch to horses for the one-hour beautiful ride to the crater rim at 1000 m. It is a further 1½ hours' walk along bare brittle lava rock to **Volcán Chico**, with several fumaroles and more stunning views. You can camp on the crater rim but must take all supplies, including water, and obtain a permit the day before from the National Park office in Puerto Villamil. A half-day tour including transport, horses and lunch costs US$40 per person (US$45 with English-speaking guide).

A visit to **Punta Moreno**, on the southwest part of the island, starts with a dinghy ride along the beautiful rocky shores where penguins and shore birds are usually seen. After a dry landing there is a hike through sharp lava rocks. **Elizabeth Bay**, on the west coast, is home to a small colony of penguins living on a series of small rocky islets and visited by dinghy. **Tagus Cove**, on the west coast across the narrow channel from Fernandina island, is an anchorage that has been used by visiting ships going back to the 1800s, and the ships' names can still be seen painted on the cliffs. A trail leads inland from Tagus Cove past Laguna Darwin, a large saltwater lake, and then further uphill to a ridge with lovely views.

Floreana Island → *Phone code: 05. Population: about 100.*

Floreana is the island with the richest human history and the fewest inhabitants, most in **Puerto Velasco Ibarra**, the rest in the highlands. Unless you visit with an organized tour or on one of the boats which land at Black Beach for a few hours, it is difficult to get onto and off the inhabited part of the island. Services are limited; you should be very flexible about travel times and self-sufficient, unless staying with the **Wittmers** or at **Lava Lodge** (see Sleeping, below). Margret Wittmer died in 2000, however, you can meet her daughter and granddaughter. The climate in the highlands is fresh and comfortable, good for birdwatching. Places to visit include the **Devil's Crown** snorkelling site, **Punta Cormorant**, a green beach near which is a lake normally inhabited by flamingos and **Post Office Bay**, on the north side. There is a custom for visitors to Post Office Bay since 1792 to place unstamped letters and cards in a barrel, and deliver, free of charge, any addressed to their own destinations.

Unpopulated islands

Bartolomé is a small island in Sullivan Bay off the eastern shore of Santiago. It is probably the most visited and most photographed of all the islands with its distinctive **Pinnacle Rock** (a trail leads to the summit). A second visitor site has a lovely beach from which you can snorkel or swim and see the penguins. **Daphne**, west of Baltra, has very rich bird-life, in particular the nesting boobies, but visits are limited to one a month. **Española** is the southernmost island of the Galápagos and, following a successful programme to remove all the feral species, it is recoveing well. Gardner Bay, on the northeastern coast, is a beautiful white sand beach with excellent swimming and snorkelling. Punta Suárez, on the western tip of the island, has a trail through a rookery. As well as a wide range of seabirds (including blue-footed and nazca boobies) there are sea lions, the largest and most colourful marine iguanas of the Galápagos and the original home of the waved albatross. **Fernadina** is the youngest of the islands, about 700,000 years old, and the most volcanically active. At Punta Espinosa, on the northeast coast, a trail goes up through a sandy nesting site for huge colonies of marine iguanas. You can also see flightless cormorants and go snorkelling in the bay.

Genovesa, at the northeast part of the archipelago, is an outpost for many sea birds. It is an eight- to 10-hour all-night sail from Puerto Ayora. Like Fernandina, Genovesa is best visited on smaller vessels with longer range; large ships are not allowed. One of the most famous sites is Prince Phillip's Steps, an amazing walk through a seabird rookery that is full of life. You will see tropicbirds, all three boobies, frigates, petrels, swallow-tailed and lava gulls, and many others. There is also good snorkelling at the foot of the steps, with lots of marine iguanas. The entrance to Darwin Bay, on the eastern side of the island, is very narrow and shallow and the anchorage in the lagoon is surrounded by mangroves, home to a large breeding colony of frigates and other seabirds.

One of the closest islands to Puerto Ayora is **Plaza Sur**. It has a combination of both dry and coastal vegetation. Walking along the sea cliffs is a pleasant experience as the swallow-tailed gull, shearwaters and red-billed tropicbirds nest here. There are also lots of blue-footed boobies and a large population of land iguanas on the island. **Rábida**, just south of Santiago, has a salt-water lagoon, occasionally home to flamingos. There is an area of mangroves near the lagoon where brown pelicans nest. You can snorkel and swim from the beach. On **Santa Fe**, between Santa Cruz and San Cristóbal, the lagoon is

Overseas agencies

Galapagos Classic Cruises, 6 Keyes Rd, London NW2 3XA, T020-8933 0613, www.galapagoscruises.co.uk. Specialists in tailor-made cruises and diving holidays to the islands with additional land tours to Ecuador and Peru on request.
Galápagos Holidays, 14 Prince Arthur Av, Suite 311, Toronto, Ontario M5R 1A9, T416-413 9090, T1-800-661 2512 (toll free), www.galapagosholidays.com.
Galápagos Network, 5805 Blue Lagoon Dr, Suite 160, Miami, FL 33126, T305-2626264, www.ecoventura.com.
INCA, 1311 63rd St, Emeryville, CA 94608, T510-420 1550, www.inca1.com.
International Expeditions, 1 Environs Park, Helena, Alabama, 35080, T205-428 1700, T1-800-633 4734, www.internationalexpeditions.com.
Select Latin America, 3.51 Canterbury Court, 1-3 Brixton Road, London SW9 6DE, T020- 7407 1478, www.selectlatinamerica.com. David Horwell arranges quality tailor-made tours to Ecuador and the Galápagos islands.
Sol International, PO Box 1738, Kodak, TN 37764, T931-536 4893, T1-800-765 5657, www.solintl.com.
Wilderness Travel, 1102 Ninth St, Berkeley, CA 94710, T510-558 2488, T1-800-368 2794, www.wildernesstravel.com.

home to a large colony of sea lions who are happy to join you for a swim. This little island has its own species of land iguana.

Santiago, a large island, also known as James, is east of Isla Isabela. It has a volcanic landscape full of cliffs and pinnacles, and is home to several species of marine birds. James Bay, on the western side of the island, has a wet landing on the dark sands of Puerto Egas. Fur sea lions are seen nearby. Espumilla Beach is another visitor site with a walk through a mangrove forest to a lake usually inhabited by flamingos, pintail ducks and stilts. Sea turtles dig their nests at the edge of the mangroves. Buccaneer Cove, in the northwest, was a haven for pirates during the 1600s and 1700s. Sullivan Bay, on the eastern coast opposite Bartolomé (see above) has a trail across an impressive lunar landscape of lava fields. Just off the southeastern tip is Sombrero Chino island, noted for its volcanic landscape. On **Seymour Norte**, just north of Baltra, the tourist trail leads through mangroves in one of the main nesting sites for blue-footed boobies and frigates in this part of the archipelago.

Galápagos Islands listings

For Sleeping and Eating price codes and other relevant information, see pages 10-11.

🔵 Sleeping

Puerto Ayora *p87*

Reservations are essential in high season.

$$$$ Finch Bay Hotel, on a small bay south of Puerto Ayora, accessible only by boat, T252 6297, www.finchbayhotel.com. A luxury hotel on a beautiful beach. Buffet breakfast, restaurant, pool, fine restaurant and bar, good service, comfortable rooms. Book through **Metropolitan Touring** in Quito.

$$$$ Red Mangrove, Darwin y las Fragatas, toward the Charles Darwin station, T252 6564, Quito T02-225 0166, www.redmangrove.com. A beautiful hotel with plenty of character, part of a group of island hotels. Includes breakfast, restaurant, jacuzzi, deck bar and lovely Japanese dining room. Very tasteful rooms all overlooking the water, ample bathrooms. Owner Hernán Rodas offers day tours and diving. Recommended.

$$$$ Royal Palm, in the highlands of Santa Cruz, T252 7409, www.royalpalmgalapagos.com. Includes breakfast, villas and suites with all luxuries, jacuzzi in rooms, private lounge at airport, part of **Millennium** international chain.

$$$$ Silberstein, Darwin y Piqueros, T252 6047, www.hotelsilberstein.com. Modern and very comfortable, with lovely grounds and a small pool, buffet breakfast, restaurant and bar, spacious rooms and common areas.

$$$$ Angemeyer Waterfront Inn, by the dock at Punta Estrada, T09-472 4955, tangermeyer@yahoo.com. Gorgeous location overlooking the bay. Includes breakfast, very comfortable modern rooms and apartments, some with kitchenettes.

$$$$ Lobo de Mar, 12 de Febrero y Darwin, T252 6188, www.lobodemar.com.ec. Modern building with balconies and rooftop terrace, great views over the harbour. Includes breakfast, a/c, 2 pools, Wi-Fi, fridge, modern and comfortable, attentive service. Recommended.

$$$$ Sol y Mar, Darwin y Binford, T252 6281, www.hotelsolymar.com.ec. Right in town but a nice location overlooking the bay. Buffet breakfast, restaurant and bar, pool and spa.

$$$ Estrella de Mar, by the water on a lane off 12 de Febrero, T252 6427. Quiet location with views over the bay. Includes breakfast, a/c, fan, fridge, spacious rooms, sitting area.

$$$ Gardner, Berlanga e Islas Plaza, T252 6979, pensiongardner@yahoo.com. Pleasant and quiet, spacious rooms, includes breakfast, a/c, older rooms with fan are cheaper, small sitting area with hammocks and outdoor cooking facilities. Recommended.

$$$ Santa Fe Suites, Charles Binford entre Juan Montalvo y Las Ninfas, T252 6419. Rooms with small kitchenettes in a quiet area, includes breakfast, fan, pool.

$$ Castro, Los Colonos y Malecón, T252 6113. Pleasant, older but well-maintained place on a quiet street. Includes breakfast, restaurant, a/c, Wi-Fi, rooftop terrace.

$$ Peregrino, Darwin e Indefatigable, T252 6323. Away from the centre of town, includes breakfast, electric shower, a/c, nice rooms, small garden, family-run, homely atmosphere.

$$ Salinas, Islas Plaza y Berlanga, T252 6107. Cheaper with cold water, fan, simple and adequate.

$ Los Amigos, Darwin y 12 de Febrero, T252 6265. Small place with a couple of 3-bed rooms, 2 rooms with private bath, cold water, laundry facilities, basic but friendly.

$ Santa Cruz, Av Baltra e Indefatigable, T252 4326. Electric shower, a/c, cheaper with fan, good value.

Puerto Baquerizo Moreno p88

$$$$ Miconia, Darwin y Melville, T252 0608, www.miconia.com. Includes breakfast, restaurant, a/c, small pool, large well-equipped gym, modern if somewhat small rooms, some with fridge.

$$$ Chatham, Northía y Av de la Armada Nacional, on the road to the airport, T252 0137, chathamhotel@hotmail.com. Patio with hammocks, meals on request, electric shower, rooms in newer section have a/c and fridge, older rooms with fan are cheaper, well maintained and nice.

$$$ Gran Hotel Mar Azul, Northía y Esmeraldas, T252 0091, www.granhotel marazul.com.ec. Modern multi-storey hotel, comfortable rooms with a/c and fridge, good service.

$$ Casablanca, Mellville y Darwin, T252 0392, jacquivaz@yahoo.com. Large white house with lovely terrace and views of harbour. Breakfast available, each room is individually decorated by the owner who has an art studio on the premises.

$$ Casa de Nelly, Northía y Roldos, T252 0112. 3-storey building in a quiet location, fan, cooking facilities, bright comfortable rooms with a fresh sea breeze.

$$ Mar Azul, Northía y Esmeraldas, T252 0139. Comfortable lodgings, electric shower, a/c, cheaper with fan, pleasant. Recommended.

$$ Suites Bellavista, Darwin y Melville, above the supermarkert, T252 0352. Good location right on the *malecón*, a/c, cooking facilities, ample modern rooms.

$ Doña Pilo, Northía y Quito, T252 0098. Electric shower, fan, family-run, simple but adequate and good value, often full.

$ León Dormido, Villamil y Darwin, T252 0169. Simple place, hot water, good value.

$ San Francisco, Darwin y Villamil, T252 0304. Cold water, fan, rooms in front are better, simple but good value.

Puerto Villamil p89

$$$$ Albemarle, on the beachfront, T252 9489, www.hotelalbemarle.com. Attractive Mediterranean-style construction, includes breakfast, a/c, bright comfortable rooms with wonderful ocean views, English/ Ecuadorean-run.

$$$$ La Casa de Marita, at east end of beach, T252 9238, www.galapagosisabela. com. Definitely upscale, even chic. Includes breakfast, other meals on request, a/c and fridge, jacuzzi, very comfortable, each room is a bit different and some have balconies. A little gem. Recommended.

$$$$ Red Mangrove, Conocarpus y Opuntia, T252 9030, www.redmangrove.com. Reception and common areas are in older wooden building, bungalows across the road are more modern, with a/c, but only the front ones have a sea view. Pricey for what it offers. Also camping in Campo Duro in the highlands.

$$$ San Vicente, Cormoranes y Pinzón Artesano, T252 9140. Very popular hotel which also offers tours and kayak rentals, includes breakfast, cold water, a/c, use of cooking facilities and fridge, meals on request, rooms a bit small but nice, camping possible, family-run. Recommended.

$$ La Casa Rosada, Antonio Gil at at west end of the beach, T252 9330, claudiahodari@ gmail.com. Nicer inside than outside, fan, terrace overlooking the ocean, comfortable rooms with antique-style furniture, fridge.

$$ Posada del Caminante, C Cormorán behind the lagoon, T252 9407. A bit out of the way, hot water, fan, ample rooms with kitchen, friendly owner.

Floreana Island, Puerto Velasco Ibarra p90

$$$$ Lava Lodge, on the beach, T252 6564, www.redmangrove.com. Part of Red Mangrove chain, includes breakfast, other meals on request, restaurant, fan when there is electricity, simple cabins. Advance booking required.

$$$$ Pensión Wittmer, right on Black Beach, T252 9506. Includes 3 delicious meals, fan when there is electricity, simple and comfortable, a very special place, reservations required.

Puerto Ayora *p87*

$$$ Angermeyer Point, across the bay, take a water-taxi from the port, T252 7007. Tue-Sat 1900-2200, Sun brunch 1100-1600. Former home of Galápagos pioneer and artist Carl Angermeyer, with his works on display. Gorgeous setting over the water (take insect repellent). Excellent, innovative and varied menu, attentive service. Reservations advised. Highly recommended.

$$$ La Dolce Italia, Charles Darwin entre Islas Plaza y 12 de Febrero. Daily 1100-1500, 1800-2200. Italian and seafood, wine list, a/c, pleasant atmosphere, attentive owner.

$$$ The Rock, Charles Darwin e Islas Plaza. 0900-2300, closed Tue. Very popular restaurant and bar, international food, sushi on Fri night.

$$$-$$ Hernán, Av Baltra y Opuntia. Daily 0730-2230. Restaurant and bar, international menu, pizza, burgers, cappuccino.

$$$-$$ La Garrapata, Charles Darwin between 12 de Febrero and Tomás de Berlanga. Mon-Sat 0900-2200, Sun 1700-2200. Good food, attractive setting and good music, juice bar, sandwiches and set lunch during the day, à la carte at night.

$$ Chocolate Galápagos, Charles Darwin entre Tomas de Berlanga y Charles Binford. Daily 0700-2200. Breakfast, snacks, meals, and desserts, outdoor seating, popular.

$ El Descanso del Guía, Charles Darwin y Los Colonos. Good-value set meals, very popular with locals.

$ Kiosks, Along Charles Binford between Padre Herrera and Rodríguez Lara. Many kiosks selling traditional food, including reasonably priced seafood. **Kiosko de Renato** is especially good; **Pelícano Goloso**, **Servi-Sabrosón** and

William also cook well. All with simple outdoor seating and a lively atmosphere, popular with locals and busy at night.

Cafés

La Casa del Lago, Moisés Brito y Juan Montalvo, Barrio Las Ninfas, a quiet area away from the main drag, www.galapagoscultural. com. Mon-Sat 0700-2200. Drinks, snacks and ice cream, live music, art and cultural activities, owners Enrique and Helena also rent apartments nearby.

Puerto Baquerizo Moreno *p88*

$$$ La Playa, Av de la Armada Nacional, by the navy base, T252 1511. Daily 0930-2330. Varied menu, fish and seafood specialities, nice location.

$$$ Miramar, on beachfront around the corner from Capitanía. Daily 1800-2400. Seafood and international dishes, variety of cocktails, lovely ocean views, great sunsets.

$$$-$$ Rosita, Ignacio de Hernández y General Villamil. Daily from 1100, closed Sun afternoon. Set meals and varied à la carte, old-time yachtie hangout.

$$ Deep Blue, Darwin y Española. Ceviches in morning, good set lunch, closed evenings. A few other simple places serve set meals.

Cafés

Mockingbird Café, Española y Hernandez. Fruit juices, brownies, snacks, internet.

Panadería Fragata, Northía y Rocafuerte. Excellent bread and pastries, good selection.

Puerto Villamil *p89*

$$ El Encanto de la Pepa, Antonio Gil on the Plaza. Set meals and à la carte, lots of character, good food, pleasant outdoor seating.

$$ La Choza, Antonio Gil y Las Fragatas. Varied menu, a bit pricey, pizza must be ordered the morning before.

$$-$ Tropical, Las Fragatas ½ block from Plaza. Open daily. Good-quality and value set meals, popular with locals.

Puerto Ayora *p87*

La Panga, Av Charles Darwin y Berlanga and **Bar Bongo**, upstairs, are both popular. **Limón y Café**, Charles Darwin y 12 de Febrero. Snacks and drinks, lots of music, pool table.

Puerto Baquerizo Moreno *p88*

Calypso, Darwin y Manuel J. Cobos, daily 1800-2400. Snacks and drinks, pleasant outdoor seating.
Iguana Rock, Quito y Juan José Flores, some live music, pool table, popular.

Puerto Villamil *p89*

Beto's Beach Bar, Antonio Gil y Los Flamencos along the beach. Pleasant location, irregular hours, very relaxed. Has a room to rent.

Most items can be purchased on the islands, but cost more than on the mainland. Do not buy items made of black coral as it is an endangered species.

Puerto Ayora *p88*

There is an attractive little **Mercado Artesanal** (craft market) at Charles Darwin y Tomás de Berlanga. **Proinsular**, opposite the pier, is the largest and best stocked supermarket.

There are various T-shirt, souvenir, and highbrow jewellery shops along the length of Av Charles Darwin, all touristy and expensive.
Camping gear Tatoo, opposite Capitanía del Puerto, T252 4101, www.tatoo.ws.

Puerto Baquerizo Moreno *p88*

Galamarket, Isabela y Juan José Flores, is a modern well-stocked supermarket. **Fabo Galería de Arte**, Malecón Charles Darwin y Melville, 2nd floor of **Hotel Casa Blanca**. Paintings by the owner Fabricio, and silk-screened T-shirts. A few souvenir shops along the Malecón sell T-shirts and crafts.

Galápagos operators on the mainland

Details of the following are given under their respective cities. **Quito** (see page 39): **Andando Tours-Angermeyer Crusies, Andean Travel Co, Andes Explorer, Creter Tours, Ecoventura, Enchanted Expeditions, Galacruises Expeditions, Galasam, Latin Trails, Mallku Expeditions, Surtrek, Zenith Travel. Guayaquil: Canodros, Galasam**. See also Choosing a tour, page 85.

Puerto Ayora *p87*

Cycling Mountain bikes can be hired from travel agencies in town. Prices and quality vary.
Diving Only specialized diving boats are allowed to do diving tours. It is not possible to dive as part of a standard live-on-board cruise. The following vessels offer live- on-board diving tours: *Agressor I and II*, www.aggressor.com; *Deep Blue*, www.deepbluegalapagosdiving.com; *Galápagos Sky*, www.ecoventura.com; *Humboldt Explorer*, www.galasam.com; and *Lammer Law*, www.quasarnautica.com. National Park rules prohibit collecting samples or souvenirs, spear-fishing, touching animals, or other environmental disruptions. Experienced dive guides can help visitors have the most spectacular opportunities to enjoy the wildlife. There are several diving agencies in Puerto Ayora, Baquerizo Moreno and Villamil offering courses, equipment rental, and dives. On offer from Puerto Ayora are dives within Academy Bay (2 dives for US$90), and other central islands (2 dives, US$140), daily tours for 1 week in the central islands. There is a hyperbaric chamber in Puerto Ayora to treat divers in case of decompression sickness (US$1500 per hr, 50% discount if your dive operator is affiliated): Rodríguez Lara y 12 de Febrero, T252 6911, www.sssnetwork.com. Confirm in advance whether your diving insurance is accepted and make sure you have adequate cover. To avoid the risk of

decompression sickness, divers are advised to stay an extra day on the islands after their last dive before flying to the mainland, especially to Quito at 2840 m above sea level.

DiveCenter Silberstein, opposite **Hotel Silberstein**, T252 6028, www.divinggalapagos. com. Trips for beginners up to PADI divemaster.

Galápagos Sub-Aqua, Av Charles Darwin e Isla Floreana, T252 6633, www.galapagos-sub- aqua.com (Guayaquil: Orellana 211 y Panamá, No 702, T04-230 5514). Mon-Sat 0800-1230, 1430-1830. Instructor Fernando Zambrano offers full certificate courses up to PADI divemaster level. Repeatedly recommended.

Nautidiving, Av Charles Darwin, T252 7004, www.nautidiving.com. Offers 8-day, 7-night trips.

Scuba Iguana, Charles Darwin near the research station, T252 6497, www.scuba iguana.com. Matías Espinoza runs this long-time reliable and recommended dive operator. Courses up to PADI divemaster.

Horse riding For riding at ranches in the highlands, enquire at **Moonrise Travel**.

Snorkelling Masks, snorkels and fins can be rented from travel agencies and dive shops, US$5 a day, deposit required. Closest place to snorkel is by beaches near Darwin Station.

Surfing There is surfing at Tortuga Bay and at other more distant beaches accessed by boat. There is better surfing near Puerto Baquerizo Moreno on San Cristóbal. The **Lonesome George** agency (see below) rents surfboards for US$10-$15 per half-day.

Tour operators
Avoid touts who approach you at the airport or in the street offering cheap tours. Also be wary of agencies who specialize in cut-rate cruises.

Lonesome George, Av Baltra y Enrique Fuentes, T252 6245, lonesomegrg@ yahoo.com. Run by Víctor Vaca. Sells tours and rents: bicycles, surf- boards, snorkelling equipment and motorcycles.

Moonrise Travel, Av Charles Darwin y Charles Binford, opposite Banco del Pacífico, T252 6348, www.galapagosmoonrise.com. Last-minute cruise bookings, day-tours to different islands, bay tours, airline reservations. Owner Jenny Devine speaks English; she is knowledgeable.

Naugala Yacht Services, Barrio El Edén, T252 7403, www.naugala.com.

Puerto Baquerizo Moreno *p88*
Cycling Hire bikes from travel agencies, US$20 per day.

Diving There are several dive sites around San Cristóbal, most popular being Kicker Rock, Roca Ballena and Punta Pitt (at the northeastern side). See Tour operators (below) who offer dives. The nearest hyperbaric chamber is in Puerto Ayora.

Surfing There is good surfing in San Cristóbal, the best season is Dec-Mar. **Punta Carola** near town is the closest surfing beach; popular among locals. There is a championship during the local fiesta, the 2nd week of Feb.

Tour operators
Chalo Tours, Española y Hernández, T252 0953. Bay tours to Kicker Rock and Isla de los Lobos, boat tours to the north end of the island, highland tours, diving tours, bike rentals, snorkelling gear, book exchange.

Galakiwi, Española y Darwin, T252 1562, galakiwi@yahoo.com.au. Owned by New-Zealander Tim Cooney. Highland and diving tours, kayaks and other gear rentals.

Sharksky, Española y Charles Darwin, T252 1188, http://sharksky.com. Adventure tours, diving, volunteering, has a popular café, helpful.

Puerto Villamil *p89*
Hotels can arrange visits to local attractions, mostly operated by Antonio Gil at **Hotel San Vicente**, reliable and recommended.

Carapachudo Tours, Escalecias y Tero Real, T252 9451, info@carapachudotours.com.

Mountain biking tours, downhill from Sierra Negra and to other attractions, US$42 for a full day including lunch. Also rentals: bikes for US$3 per hr, US$20 per day; surf boards US$4 per hr.

Isabela Dive Center, Escalecia y Alberto Gil, T252 9418, www.isabeladivecenter.com.ec. Diving, land and boat tours.

🚌 Transport

Puerto Ayora p87

Pick-ups may be hired for transport throughout town, US$1-2, agree fare in advance. Up to the highlands, they leave throughout the day from in front of the Tropidurus store, Av Baltra corner Jaime Roldos, 2 blocks past the market: to **Bellavista** US$0.25, 10 mins; to **Santa Rosa** US$1, 20 mins; to **Playa Garrapatero** US$30 for the vehicle round trip including wait. **Water taxis** (*taxis marítimos*) from the pier to anchored boats and Punta Estrada, US$0.60 pp from 0600 until 1900 and then US$1. Several taxis work until midnight. There is always one on duty 24-hr but you might have to wait awhile when lots of boats are in port, especially Fri and Sat. If you have access, call them on channel 14.

ℹ️ Directory

Puerto Ayora p87

Airline offices Aerogal, Rodríguez Lara y San Cristóbal, T252 6798. **TAME**, Av Charles Darwin y 12 de Febrero, T252 6527. **Emetebe**, Av Charles Darwin near port, 2nd floor of Ferroinsular hardware store next to Proinsular supermarket, T252 6177. **Banks** Banco del Pacífico, Av Charles Darwin y Charles Binford, T252 6282, Mon-Fri 0800-1530, Sat 0930-1230. US$5 commission per transaction for TCs, maximum US$500 per transaction. ATM works with Cirrus, Plus and MC but not Visa; cash advances from tellers on Visa and MC. **Embassies and consulates** British Consul, David Balfour, T252 6159. **Medical services** Hospitals: there is a hospital on Av Baltra for first aid and basic care. For anything serious, locals usually fly to the mainland. Also

see hyperbaric chamber under Diving, above. **Internet** There are several cybercafés throughout town, US$2 per hr. **Post offices** By the port, sometimes has commemorative Galápagos stamps; unreliable, it often runs out of stamps, never leave money and letters. **DHL courier and Western Union**, across the street from Hotel Silberstein. **Useful addresses** Yacht agents Galapagos Ocean Services (Peter Schiess), Charles Darwin next to Garrapata restaurant, T09-477 0804, www.gos.ec. **Naugala Yacht Services** (Jhonny Romero), T252 7403, www.naugala.com.

Puerto Baquerizo Moreno p14

Airline offices Aerogal, at the airport, T252 1118. **TAME**, Charles Darwin y Manuel J Cobos, T252 1351, airport counter T252 1089. **Emetebe**, at the airport T252 0615. **Banks** Banco del Pacífico, Charles Darwin entre Española y Melville. Same hours and services as in Puerto Ayora. **Internet** US$2 per hr. **Laundry** Lavandería Limpio y Seco, Av Northía y 12 de Febrero. Wash and dry US$2. Open daily 0900- 2100. **Medical services** There is a hospital providing only basic medical services. **Dr David Basantes**, opposite Hotel Mar Azul, T252 0126, is a helpful GP. **Farmacia San Cristóbal**, Villamil y Hernández. **Post offices** Malecón Charles Darwin y 12 de Febrero.

Puerto Villamil p89

Airline offices Emetebe, Antonio Gil y Las Fragatas, T252 9155. **Banks** There are no banks on Isabela, no ATMs, and nowhere to use credit cards or change TCs. You must bring US$ cash. **Money Gram**, Terro Real y Escalecias, in Hotel Insular, for international funds transfer. If stuck without funds, ask Emetebe if they can give cash against Visa or MasterCard; it may take a day or 2 for the cash to arrive. **Internet** There are a couple of slow cybercafés in town, US$2 per hr.

Contents

Footnotes

Basic Spanish for travellers

Spanish words

Basics

bank	el banco	expensive	caro/a
bathroom/toilet	el baño	market	el mercado
bill	la factura/la cuenta	note/coin	le billete/la moneda
cash	el efectivo	police (policeman)	la policía (el policía)
cheap	barato/a	post office	el correo
credit card	la tarjeta de crédito	public telephone	el teléfono público
exchange house	la casa de cambio	supermarket	el supermercado
exchange rate	el tipo de cambio	ticket office	la taquilla

Getting around

airport	el aeropuerto	highway, main road	la carretera
arrival/departure	la llegada/salida	insurance	el seguro
avenue	la avenida	insured person	el/la asegurado/a
block	la cuadra	to insure yourself against	asegurarse contra
border	la frontera	luggage	el equipaje
bus station	la terminal de autobuses/camiones	north, south, west, east	norte, sur, oeste (occidente), este (oriente)
bus	el bus/el autobús/el camión	passport	el pasaporte
		street	la calle
collective/ fixed-route taxi	el colectivo	that way	por allí/por allá
corner	la esquina	this way	por aquí/por acá
first/second class	primera/segunda clase	tourist card/visa	la tarjeta de turista
left/right	izquierda/derecha	tyre	la llanta
ticket	el boleto	to walk	caminar/andar
empty/full	vacío/lleno		

Accommodation

air conditioning	el aire acondicionado	power cut	el apagón/corte
all-inclusive	todo incluido	restaurant	el restaurante
bathroom, private	el baño privado	room/bedroom	el cuarto/la habitación
bed, double/single	la cama matrimonial/sencilla	sheets	las sábanas
		shower	la ducha/regadera
blankets	las cobijas/mantas	soap	el jabón
to clean	limpiar	toilet	el sanitario/excusado
dining room	el comedor	toilet paper	el papel higiénico
guesthouse	la casa de huéspedes	towels, clean/dirty	las toallas limpias/sucias
hotel	el hotel		
noisy	ruidoso	water, hot/cold	el agua caliente/fría
pillows	las almohadas		

Health

aspirin	*la aspirina*	pain	*el dolor*
blood	*la sangre*	head	*la cabeza*
chemist	*la farmacia*	period/sanitary towels	*la regla/*
contact lenses	*los lentes de contacto*		*las toallas femeninas*
diarrhoea	*la diarrea*	stomach	*el estómago*
doctor	*el médico*	altitude sickness	*el soroche*
fever/sweat	*la fiebre/el sudor*		

Days and time

Monday	*lunes*	at a quarter to three	*a cuarto para las tres/*
Tuesday	*martes*		*a las tres menos quince*
Wednesday	*miércoles*	it's one o'clock	*es la una*
Thursday	*jueves*	it's seven o'clock	*son las siete*
Friday	*viernes*	it's six twenty	*son las seis y veinte*
Saturday	*sábado*	it's five to nine	*son las nueve menos*
Sunday	*domingo*		*cinco*
		in ten minutes	*en diez minutos*
at one o'clock	*a la una*	five hours	*cinco horas*
at half past two	*a las dos y media*	does it take long?	*¿tarda mucho?*

Numbers

one	*uno/una*	sixteen	*dieciséis*
two	*dos*	seventeen	*diecisiete*
three	*tres*	eighteen	*dieciocho*
four	*cuatro*	nineteen	*diecinueve*
five	*cinco*	twenty	*veinte*
six	*seis*	twenty-one	*veintiuno*
seven	*siete*	thirty	*treinta*
eight	*ocho*	forty	*cuarenta*
nine	*nueve*	fifty	*cincuenta*
ten	*diez*	sixty	*sesenta*
eleven	*once*	seventy	*setenta*
twelve	*doce*	eighty	*ochenta*
thirteen	*trece*	ninety	*noventa*
fourteen	*catorce*	hundred	*cien/ciento*
fifteen	*quince*	thousand	*mil*

Food

avocado	*la palta*	beef	*la carne de res*
baked	*al horno*	beef steak	*el lomo*
bakery	*la panadería*	boiled rice	*el arroz blanco*
banana	*la banana*	bread	*el pan*
beans	*los frijoles/*	breakfast	*el desayuno*
	las habichuelas	butter	*la manteca*

cake	*la torta*	onion	*la cebolla*
chewing gum	*el chicle*	orange	*la naranja*
chicken	*el pollo*	pepper	*el pimiento*
chilli or green pepper	*el ají/pimiento*	pasty, turnover	*la empanada/*
clear soup, stock	*el caldo*		*el pastelito*
cooked	*cocido*	pork	*el cerdo*
dining room	*el comedor*	potato	*la papa*
egg	*el huevo*	prawns	*los camarones*
fish	*el pescado*	raw	*crudo*
fork	*el tenedor*	restaurant	*el restaurante*
fried	*frito*	salad	*la ensalada*
garlic	*el ajo*	salt	*la sal*
goat	*el chivo*	sandwich	*el bocadillo*
grapefruit	*la toronja/el pomelo*	sauce	*la salsa*
grill	*la parrilla*	sausage	*la longaniza/el chorizo*
grilled/griddled	*a la plancha*	scrambled eggs	*los huevos revueltos*
guava	*la guayaba*	seafood	*los mariscos*
ham	*el jamón*	soup	*la sopa*
hamburger	*la hamburguesa*	spoon	*la cuchara*
hot, spicy	*picante*	squash	*la calabaza*
ice cream	*el helado*	squid	*los calamares*
jam	*la mermelada*	supper	*la cena*
knife	*el cuchillo*	sweet	*dulce*
lemon	*el limón*	to eat	*comer*
lobster	*la langosta*	toasted	*tostado*
lunch	*el almuerzo/la comida*	turkey	*el pavo*
meal	*la comida*	vegetables	*los legumbres/vegetales*
meat	*la carne*	without meat	*sin carne*
minced meat	*la carne picada*	yam	*el camote*

Drink

beer	*la cerveza*	ice/without ice	*el hielo/sin hielo*
boiled	*hervido/a*	juice	*el jugo*
bottled	*en botella*	lemonade	*la limonada*
camomile tea	*la manzanilla*	milk	*la leche*
canned	*en lata*	mint	*la menta*
coffee	*el café*	rum	*el ron*
coffee, white	*el café con leche*	soft drink	*el refresco*
cold	*frío*	sugar	*el azúcar*
cup	*la taza*	tea	*el té*
drink	*la bebida*	to drink	*beber/tomar*
drunk	*borracho/a*	water	*el agua*
firewater	*el aguardiente*	water, carbonated	*el agua mineral con gas*
fruit milkshake	*el batido/licuado*	water, still mineral	*el agua mineral sin gas*
glass	*el vaso*	wine, red	*el vino tinto*
hot	*caliente*	wine, white	*el vino blanco*

Index

Titles available in the Footprint *Focus* range

Latin America	UK RRP	US RRP
Bahia & Salvador	£7.99	$11.95
Buenos Aires & Pampas	£7.99	$11.95
Costa Rica	£8.99	$12.95
Cuzco, La Paz & Lake Titicaca	£8.99	$12.95
El Salvador	£5.99	$8.95
Guadalajara & Pacific Coast	£6.99	$9.95
Guatemala	£8.99	$12.95
Guyana, Guyane & Suriname	£5.99	$8.95
Havana	£6.99	$9.95
Honduras	£7.99	$11.95
Nicaragua	£7.99	$11.95
Paraguay	£5.99	$8.95
Quito & Galápagos Islands	£7.99	$11.95
Recife & Northeast Brazil	£7.99	$11.95
Rio de Janeiro	£8.99	$12.95
São Paulo	£5.99	$8.95
Uruguay	£6.99	$9.95
Venezuela	£8.99	$12.95
Yucatán Peninsula	£6.99	$9.95

Asia	UK RRP	US RRP
Angkor Wat	£5.99	$8.95
Bali & Lombok	£8.99	$12.95
Chennai & Tamil Nadu	£8.99	$12.95
Chiang Mai & Northern Thailand	£7.99	$11.95
Goa	£6.99	$9.95
Hanoi & Northern Vietnam	£8.99	$12.95
Ho Chi Minh City & Mekong Delta	£7.99	$11.95
Java	£7.99	$11.95
Kerala	£7.99	$11.95
Kolkata & West Bengal	£5.99	$8.95
Mumbai & Gujarat	£8.99	$12.95

Africa	UK RRP	US RRP
Beirut	£6.99	$9.95
Damascus	£5.99	$8.95
Durban & KwaZulu Natal	£8.99	$12.95
Fès & Northern Morocco	£8.99	$12.95
Jerusalem	£8.99	$12.95
Johannesburg & Kruger National Park	£7.99	$11.95
Kenya's beaches	£8.99	$12.95
Kilimanjaro & Northern Tanzania	£8.99	$12.95
Zanzibar & Pemba	£7.99	$11.95

Europe	UK RRP	US RRP
Bilbao & Basque Region	£6.99	$9.95
Granada & Sierra Nevada	£6.99	$9.95
Málaga	£5.99	$8.95
Orkney & Shetland Islands	£5.99	$8.95
Skye & Outer Hebrides	£6.99	$9.95

North America	UK RRP	US RRP
Vancouver & Rockies	£8.99	$12.95

Australasia	UK RRP	US RRP
Brisbane & Queensland	£8.99	$12.95
Perth	£7.99	$11.95

For the latest books, e-books and smart phone app releases, and a wealth of travel information, visit us at: www.footprinttravelguides.com.

footprinttravelguides.com

Join us on facebook for the latest travel news, product releases, offers and amazing competitions: www.facebook. com/footprintbooks.com.